Best Editorial Cartoons of the Year

BEST EDITORIAL CARTOONS OF THE YEAR

1983 EDITION

Edited by
CHARLES BROOKS

Foreword by JAMES WATT

PELICAN PUBLISHING COMPANY
GRETNA 1983

Special acknowledgement is made to the following for permission to use copyrighted material in this volume:

Editorial cartoons by Richard Allison, © Army Times; Bob Beckett, © New Jersey Newspapers; Jim Berry, © NEA; Vic Cantone, © New York Daily News and Rothco; Paul Conrad, © Los Angeles Times Syndicate; Tom Darcy © Newsday; Art Henrikson, © Paddock Publications; Kevin Kallaugher, © K. K. Syndication Service; Michael Konopacki, © Press Associates, Inc.; Al Liederman, © Rothco; Jimmy Margulies, © Rothco; David Wiley Miller, © Copley News Service; Jim Orton, © Computerworld; Eldon Pletcher, © Rothco; Jerry Robinson, © Cartoonists and Writers Syndicate; John Stampone, © AFL-CIO News; Art Wood, © Farm Bureau News; Bob Zschiesche, © Bob Zschiesche Cartoons; Gary Huck, © Rothco; Bill de Ore, © Field Syndicate; Dick Locher, © Chicago Tribune—New York News Syndicate; Bill Garner, © United Features Syndicate; Mike Peters, © United Features Syndicate; Lee Judge, © Field Syndicate; and John Trever, © Field Syndicate.

Library of Congress Serial Catalog Data

Best editorial cartoons. 1972-
    Gretna [La.] Pelican Pub. Co.
    v. 29cm. annual-
"A pictorial history of the year."

    I. United States- Politics and government—
1969—Caricatures and Cartoons—Periodicals.
E839.5.B45   320.9'7309240207   73-643645
ISSN 0091-2220   MARC-S

Manufactured in the United States of America

Published by Pelican Publishing Company, Inc.
1101 Monroe Street, Gretna, Louisiana 70053

Designed by Barney McKee ·

Contents

Foreword

In case you don't recognize the name, I am that fellow who has graced so many editorial pages—the one with the oil derricks growing out of his bald head, carrying the chainsaw, driving the bulldozer, shooting Smokey the Bear, and bagging Santa's reindeer. I am the man with the big smile and thick glasses who provided such an easy target for the cartoonists of the early 1980s.

Perhaps no one knows better than I how much creative or devastating power cartoonists have at their command. They can entertain us, enrage us, ennoble us, and demean and demoralize us. They can enrich and unite America, or divide and enfeeble it. Through their pens, they can elevate the obscure to greatness, and they can topple the mighty. Truly, one cartoon can have greater impact than thousands of well-chosen words.

In a matter of weeks, the cartoonists of America helped transform this rather obscure Denver lawyer and former government official into one of the most controversial figures in America. Cartoonists portrayed me as a steam shovel, chainsaw, bulldozer, owl, snake, fox, vulture, cat, whale, and Darth Vader. They showed me cutting down Winnie the Pooh's treehouse, attacking Yogi Bear with a chainsaw, skewering Bambi, and as the subject of fearful discussions among the many animals of the forest.

Sometimes I had to run to the mirror to make sure I had not been transformed into one of their creations. After seeing all the dreadful things the cartoonists showed me doing to the environment, I had to check regularly to see that the sun was still shining, the rivers were still flowing, the mountains were still standing. They were. And they are.

The cartoonists even influenced my family. After several months of merciless cartoons, my mother called from Denver to ask why I had changed from the loving, friendly, and thoughtful son she once had known. Suddenly I knew what it was to have a face that would launch a thousand cartoons.

One thing I quickly found was that cartoons—even those that are highly critical and grossly unfair—cut two ways. Jim Watt became a negative symbol to those who insist upon a no-growth, back-to-nature, preservation-first philosophy of resource management. At the same

FOREWORD

time Jim Watt became the champion of those people who believe in a balanced approach to conservation so that America can achieve economic recovery, provide jobs, advance equality, and improve national security. Cartoonists who ridiculed me for my advocacy of sound stewardship principles provided the billboards to rally those who believe as I do.

Past secretaries of the interior have never been in great demand as speakers, but suddenly everyone wanted me to address their association, convention, or other event. The cartoons served to excite interest among those who share my concern for stewardship and my opposition to blind preservationism.

In effect I gave cartoonists something to draw—and they made me a drawing card.

Cartoonists are a major force in creating the images that help define life, whether those images reflect truth or not. So they have a grave responsibility for their work. At the same time, the cartoons—the funny, the supportive, the critical, and even the grossly unfair ones—have helped me keep my perspective. They have reminded me that although I must take my work and my principles very seriously, I must not take myself too seriously.

I enjoy this wonderful art, and I know that readers will delight in this collection of cartoons.

JAMES WATT
Secretary of the Interior

Award–Winning Cartoons

1982 PULITZER PRIZE

BEN SARGENT
Editorial Cartoonist
Austin American-Statesman

Born in Amarillo, Texas, in 1948 to a newspaper family; learned print-ing trade at age 12 and began newspaper career at 14; earned journalism degree from the University of Texas at Austin, 1970; worked as politi-cal reporter for *Corpus Christi Caller-Times*, the Long News Service, United Press International, and the *Austin American-Statesman*; began drawing editorial cartoons, 1974; work distributed nationally by United Features Syndicate.

1982 NATIONAL HEADLINERS
CLUB AWARD

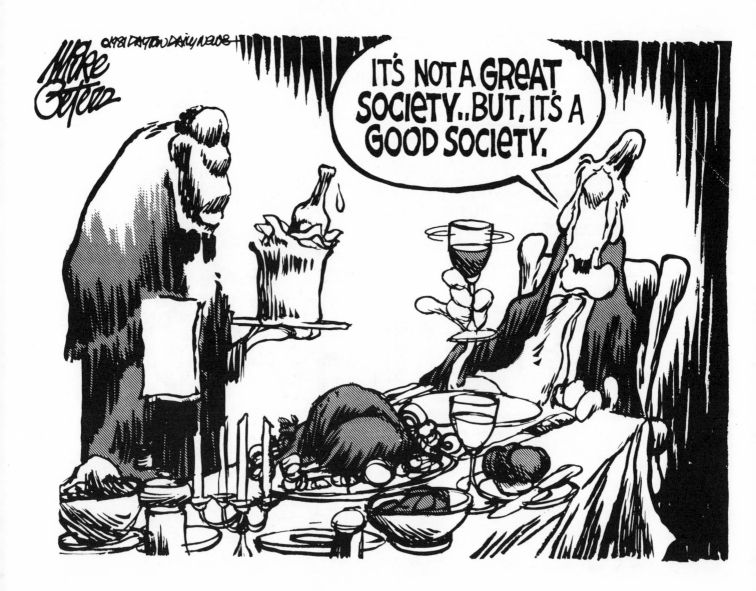

MIKE PETERS
Editorial Cartoonist
Dayton Daily News

Born 1943 in St. Louis; graduated from Washington University, 1965; cartoonist for *Chicago Daily News*, 1965; U.S. Army artist in Okinawa, 1966-67; *Chicago Daily News*, 1967-69; editorial cartoonist for the *Dayton Daily News*, 1969 to present; cartoons syndicated by United Features Syndicate; winner of Sigma Delta Chi Award for cartooning, 1975; Overseas Press Award, 1976; Distinguished Alumni Award by Washington University, 1981.

1981 SIGMA DELTA CHI AWARD
(Selected in 1982)

"YOU DON'T LOOK TRULY NEEDY TO ME ... NEEDY PERHAPS, BUT NOT TRULY NEEDY!"

PAUL CONRAD
Editorial Cartoonist
Los Angeles Times

Editorial cartoonist for the *Denver Post* for fourteen years; chief editorial cartoonist for the *Los Angeles Times*, 1964 to present; Pulitzer Prize for editorial cartoons, 1964 and 1971; winner of three awards for cartooning excellence by Sigma Delta Chi, 1962, 1970, 1980; Overseas Press Club Award, 1980; cartoons distributed by the Los Angeles Times Syndicate.

1982 JOHN FISCHETTI AWARD

WHEN RONALD REAGAN TALKS...

LEE JUDGE
Editorial Cartoonist
Kansas City Times

Born May 3, 1953, in Roseville, California; commercial artist, 1971-78; staff cartoonist and artist, *Sacramento Union*, 1978; editorial cartoonist, *San Diego Union*, 1979-80; editorial cartoonist, *Kansas City Times* and *Star*, 1981 to present; previously syndicated by Copley News Service and Field Newspaper Syndicate; first recipient of the award named in honor of John Fischetti, longtime editorial cartoonist for the *Chicago Sun-Times* who died in 1980.

1981 NATIONAL NEWSPAPER AWARD/CANADA
(Selected in 1982)

TOM INNES
Editorial Cartoonist
Calgary Herald

Editorial cartoonist for the *Calgary Herald* for twenty-five years; widely known for his incisive commentary on Canadian government affairs.

Best Editorial Cartoons of the Year

ED STEIN
Courtesy Rocky Mountain News

14

The Reagan Administration

President Reagan ran into trouble with his new Federalism plan introduced in his January State of the Union address. The plan called for transferring the responsibility for many social programs to the states in exchange for the federal government's taking over Medicaid. State officials howled, as they feared they would get less revenue.

U.S. relations with European allies chilled when Reagan slapped an embargo on their shipments of equipment needed to build a natural gas pipeline from Russia to Western Europe. The countries involved defied the ban; it was eventually lifted by Reagan in November.

The president campaigned for Republican candidates in more than a dozen states prior to the November elections. He pointed to a decline in inflation and in interest rates, which he maintained had occurred because of his economic program. He urged voters to "stay the course." The Democrats gained twenty-six House seats, thus setting the stage for a difficult future for Reaganomics.

JACK OHMAN
Courtesy Detroit Free Press

PAUL CONRAD
Courtesy Los Angeles Times

"I DON'T KNOW WHO YOU ARE, BUT YOU HAVEN'T SAID A WORD THAT'S TRUE YET....SO SHUT UP!"

PRESS ASSOCIATES INC.

MICHAEL KONOPACKI
© Press Associates, Inc.

JIM BORGMAN
Courtesy Cincinnati Enquirer

"RELAX, SAM ....DON'T YOU REMEMBER THAT CHANGING COURSE WAS CARTER'S BIG MISTAKE?"

ART BIMROSE
Courtesy The Oregonian

GEORGE FISHER
Courtesy Arkansas Gazette

H. CLAY BENNETT
Courtesy St. Petersburg Times

N.E.R.

ETTA HULME
Courtesy Ft. Worth Star–Telegram

CHAN LOWE
Courtesy Oklahoma City Times

WELL...IT WAS A TAXING IDEA.

"Been waiting long?"

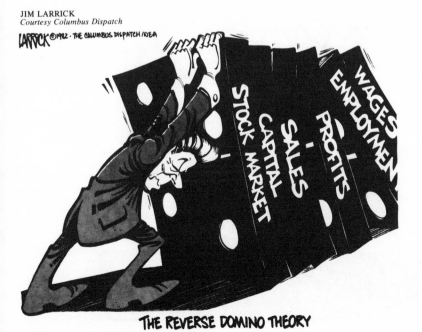

THE REVERSE DOMINO THEORY

KARL HUBENTHAL
Courtesy Los Angeles Herald–Examiner

BLAINE
Courtesy The Spectator (Ont.)

BOB TAYLOR
Courtesy Dallas Times–Herald

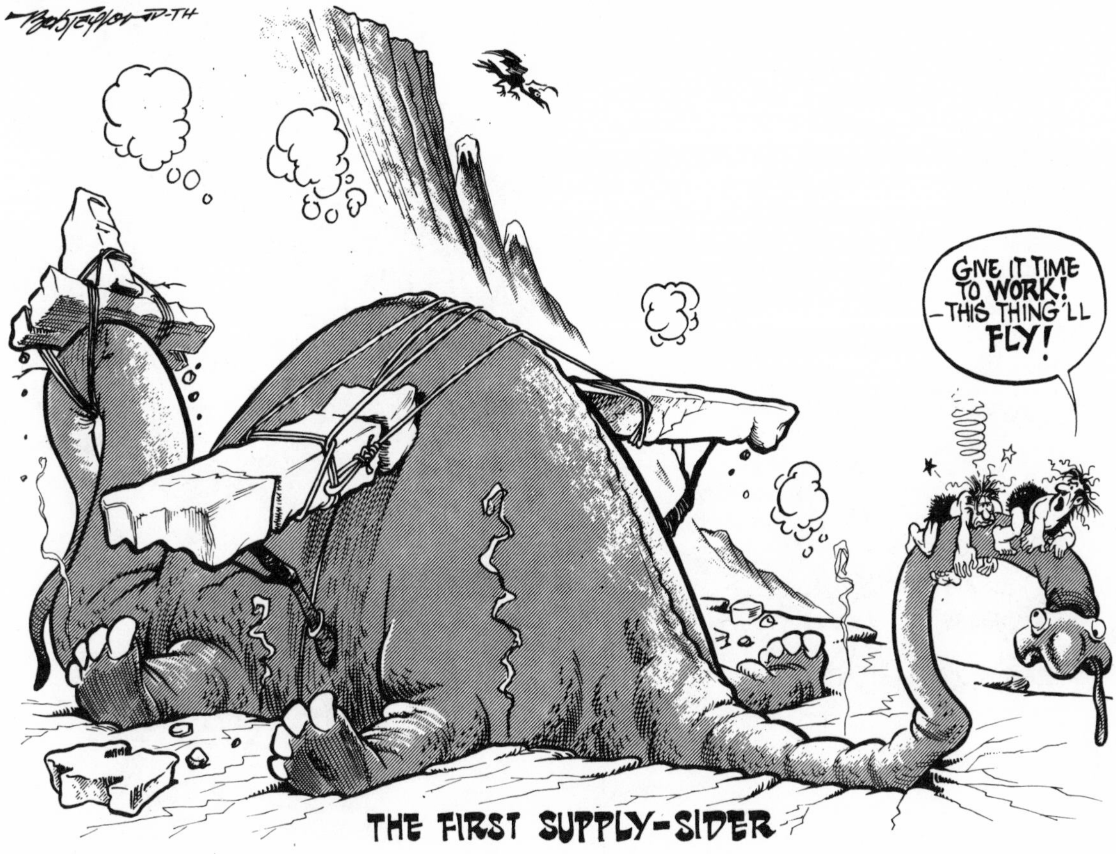
GIVE IT TIME TO WORK! —THIS THING'LL FLY!
THE FIRST SUPPLY-SIDER

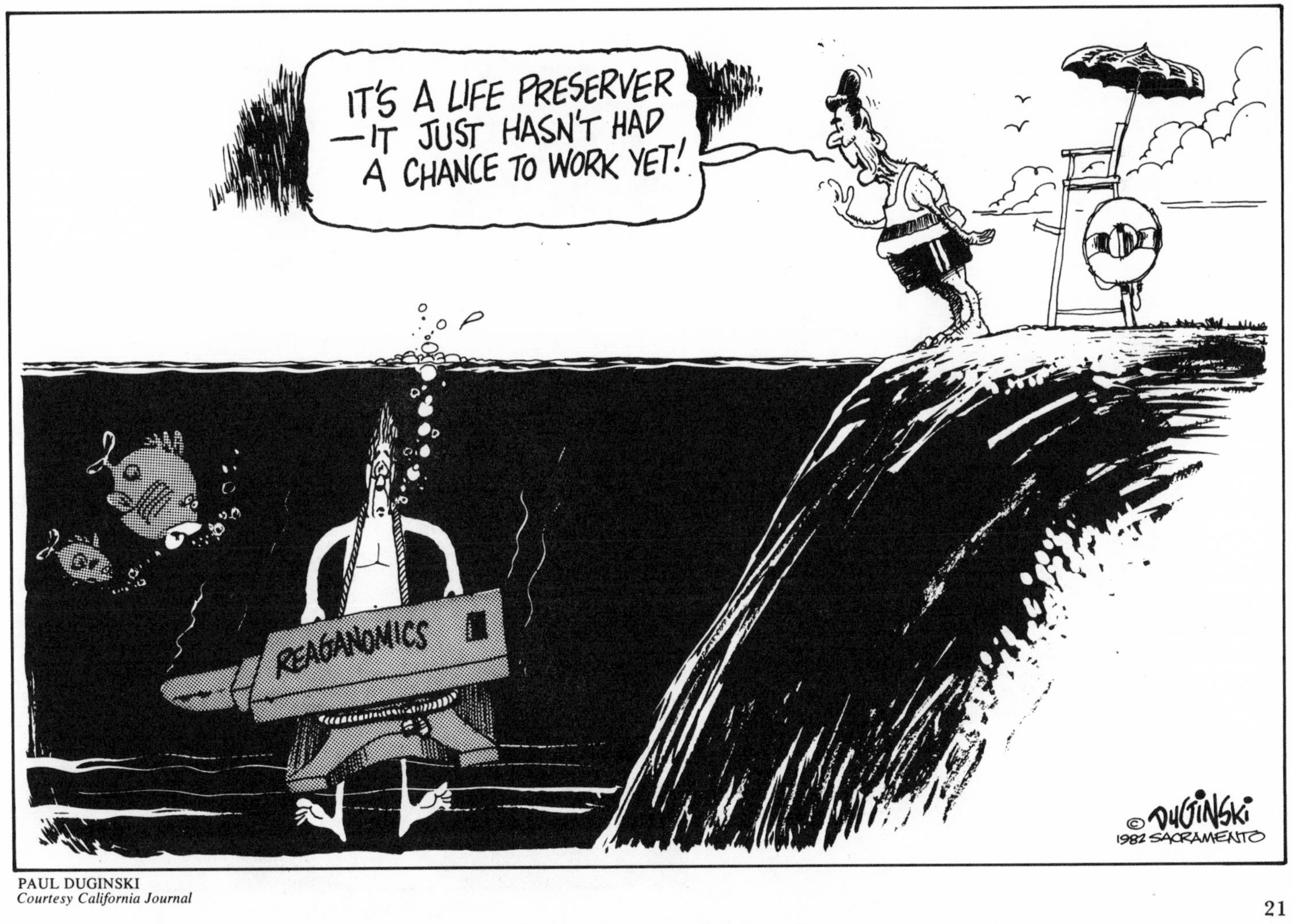
IT'S A LIFE PRESERVER —IT JUST HASN'T HAD A CHANCE TO WORK YET!
REAGANOMICS
© DUGINSKI 1982 SACRAMENTO

PAUL DUGINSKI
Courtesy California Journal

'You Gotta Be Kidding!'

JOHN STAMPONE
Courtesy AFL–CIO News

LAZARO FRESQUET
Courtesy El Miami Herald

CORKY
Courtesy Honolulu Star–Bulletin

DENNIS RENAULT
Courtesy Sacramento Bee

"As our first Republican president said, 'You may employ all of the people some of the time; you can even employ some of the people all of the time; but you can't employ all of the people all of the time.'"

ROY CARLESS
Courtesy Steel Labor, VE News

"Nothing to it. All you have to do is push"

FLIP   FLOP   FLIP   FLOP!

"The bad news is we're lost. The GOOD news is it's all CARTER'S fault!"

BILL SANDERS
Courtesy Milwaukee Journal

THE REAGAN SAFETY NET

JERRY FEARING
*Courtesy St. Paul Dispatch–
Pioneer Press*

EDDIE GERMANO
Courtesy Brockton Daily Enterprise

JOHN TREVER
Courtesy Albuquerque Journal

U.S. Budget

The latest budget deficit forecast for 1983 hovered around $200 billion, with no improvement in sight for several years to come.

The hemorrhage in the federal budget was caused by huge losses in tax receipts due to the prolonged recession, and by the resulting increased spending on unemployment compensation. President Reagan's individual and business tax cuts, initiated in 1981 and totaling some $750 billion over five years, also eroded tax revenues.

Congressional and private analysts predict deficits in the $150 billion range over the next few years, and some experts forecast even greater amounts of red ink.

A compromise tax increase package calling for tax increases of $98.3 billion and spending cuts of $30.8 billion over three years passed Congress. Reagan lobbied actively for this compromise and contended that most of the new taxes were in the form of loophole closing.

The 1983 budget showed an increase of 18 percent in military spending. Domestic spending, however, took the lion's share of the budget.

DICK LOCHER
Courtesy Chicago Tribune

JON KENNEDY
Courtesy Arkansas Democrat

Budgetshop Quartet

FRANK EVERS
Courtesy New York Daily News

DAVID HORSEY
Courtesy Seattle Post–Intelligencer

BEN SARGENT
Courtesy Austin American–Statesman

DWANE POWELL
Courtesy News & Observer (N.C.)

BILL GARNER
Courtesy Commercial Appeal (Memphis)

STEVE SACK
Courtesy Minneapolis Tribune

BILL SANDERS
Courtesy Milwaukee Journal

STEVE SACK
Courtesy Minneapolis Tribune

JOHN TREVER
Courtesy Albuquerque Journal

PAT CROWLEY
Courtesy The Post (W. Palm Beach)

U.S. Congress

Congress took a politically dangerous step in an election year by voting a massive tax increase into law. After a period of intense debate the bulk of President Reagan's 1983 budget, based on cutbacks in many social programs and an increase in defense spending, was accepted. Republicans were supported in most of the president's proposals during the year by the so-called boll weevils—Democrats who consistently voted with the GOP.

Throughout the summer Reagan put his personal prestige behind a proposed constitutional amendment that would prohibit federal spending in excess of revenues—except in wartime or with a three-fifths vote of both houses of Congress. However, the House killed the measure on September 30.

Sen. Jesse Helms of North Carolina led drives on social issues—one to ban federal funds for abortion and the other to permit school prayer. Both were defeated in the Senate.

Because of the massacres of Palestinian refugees in Lebanon, Congress voted to keep military aid to Israel at the fiscal 1982 level. The status quo was also maintained for aid to other countries.

A six-month investigation of Secretary of Labor Raymond Donovan yielded insufficient evidence to warrant prosecution on criminal corruption charges.

Baldy

CLIFF BALDOWSKI
Courtesy Atlanta Constitution

JACK MCLEOD
Courtesy Buffalo Evening News

JOEL PETT
*Courtesy Bloomington
Herald–Telephone*

32

JIM BERRY
©NEA

JACK-IN-THE BOX

ART WOOD
Courtesy AFBF (Md.)

'**GOOD HEAVENS - BOOZE!** I WONDER HOW IT GOT IN THERE...'

ED ASHLEY
Courtesy Toledo Blade

33

CLYDE PETERSON
Courtesy Houston Chronicle

'You should be grateful — lookit all the bloat you've lost!'

DANI AGUILA
Courtesy Filipino Reporter

TOM ENGELHARDT
Courtesy St. Louis Post–Dispatch

JOHN GARCIA
Courtesy Millbrae (Calif.) Sun

'Mr. Congressman, I Realize This Was Only Supposed
To Be A Cushion For My Retirement Years . . .'

LAMBERT DER
Courtesy Raleigh Times

BOB ENGLEHART
Courtesy Hartford Courant

JACK OHMAN
Courtesy Detroit Free Press

MIKE KEEFE
Courtesy Denver Post

National Defense

President Reagan called upon Congress to approve a defense budget of $221.1 billion, and the solons virtually matched his request in their lame-duck session.

The MX land-based intercontinental ballistic missile continued to be a source of controversy. Congress first okayed production of five MXs, then delayed funding until President Reagan devised a permanent basing plan. Exactly how the MX would be deployed was still undecided at year's end.

The largest anti-nuclear rally in history was held in New York City on June 15; the event drew 700,000 participants. Its purpose was to draw attention to the enormous number of nuclear weapons worldwide and to advocate a freeze in the size of the U.S.—Soviet arsenal. The president contended such a freeze would favor Russia. Reagan did propose that the U.S. and the Soviet Union begin a new series of strategic arms reduction talks. The negotiations got under way in Geneva on June 29.

The volunteer army appeared in good shape. Because jobs were increasingly hard to come by, all armed services experienced no trouble in getting all the recruits they needed.

TOM FLANNERY
Courtesy Baltimore Sun

"Sounds Like a Sinister Foreign Movement to Me"

OLLIE HARRINGTON
Courtesy N.Y. Daily World

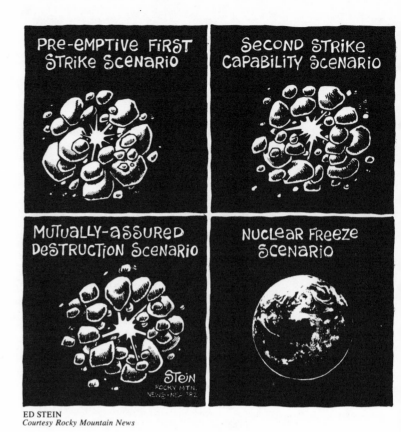

ED STEIN
Courtesy Rocky Mountain News

ETTA HULME
Courtesy Ft. Worth Star–Telegram

"THE BEAUTY OF OUR POSITION IS THAT IF THEY SHOULD HAPPEN TO BE RIGHT, THEY WON'T BE AROUND TO SAY 'I TOLD YOU SO'"

CHUCK ASAY
Courtesy Colorado Springs Sun

Calling to get peace in the neighborhood

CHUCK BROOKS
Courtesy Birmingham News

'You'll Not Get Rich (Rat-Tattatta-Tat) You're In The Arms Race Now!'

CHARLES BISSELL
Courtesy The Tennessean

JIM BORGMAN
Courtesy Cincinnati Enquirer

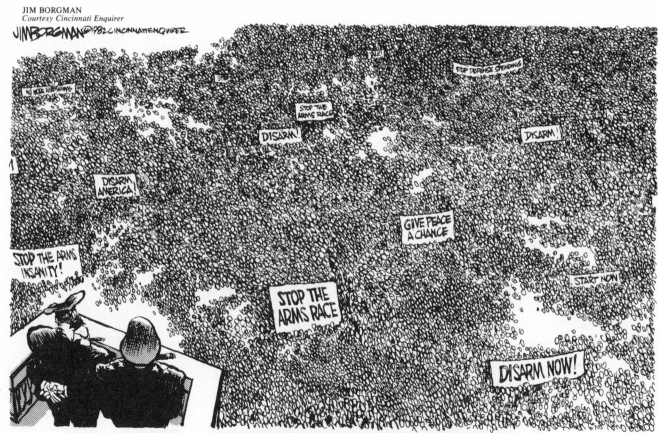

"OH, SURE, YOU'LL ALWAYS HAVE YOUR FRINGE ELEMENT..."

ADMINISTRATION'S CIVIL DEFENSE PLAN FOR NUCLEAR WAR

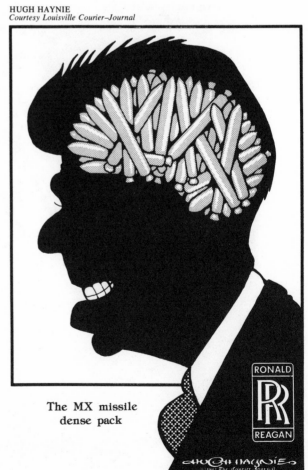

The MX missile
dense pack

JOHN TREVER
Courtesy Albuquerque Journal

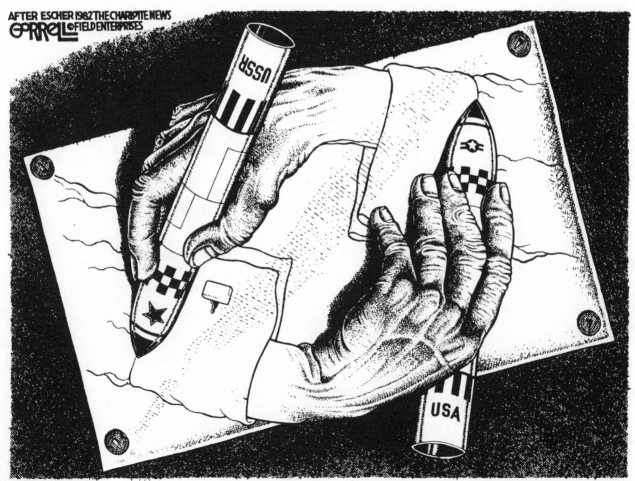

BOB GORRELL
Courtesy Charlotte News

KATE SALLEY PALMER
Courtesy Greenville News

JIM MAZZOTTA
Ft. Myers News–Press

"HE'S GOT TO EAT TO HAVE THE STRENGTH TO START REDUCING..."

"Well, another survivor of the nuclear war. Hi, I'm your new mailthing"

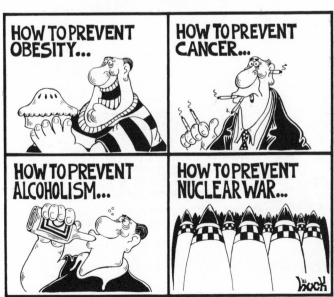

GARY HUCK
Courtesy Racine Labor

KEN ALEXANDER
Courtesy San Francisco Examiner

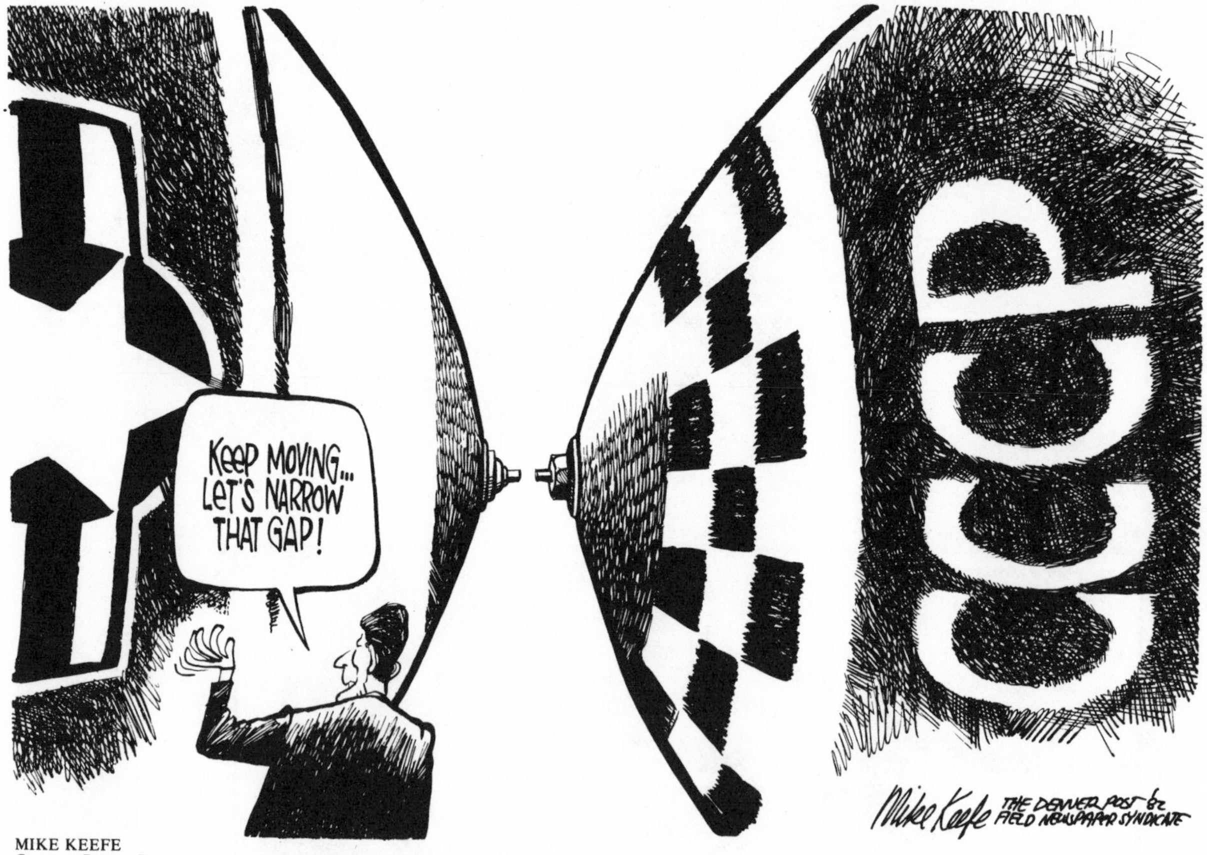
KEEP MOVING... LET'S NARROW THAT GAP!
Mike Keefe THE DENVER POST '82 FIELD NEWSPAPER SYNDICATE

MIKE KEEFE
Courtesy Denver Post

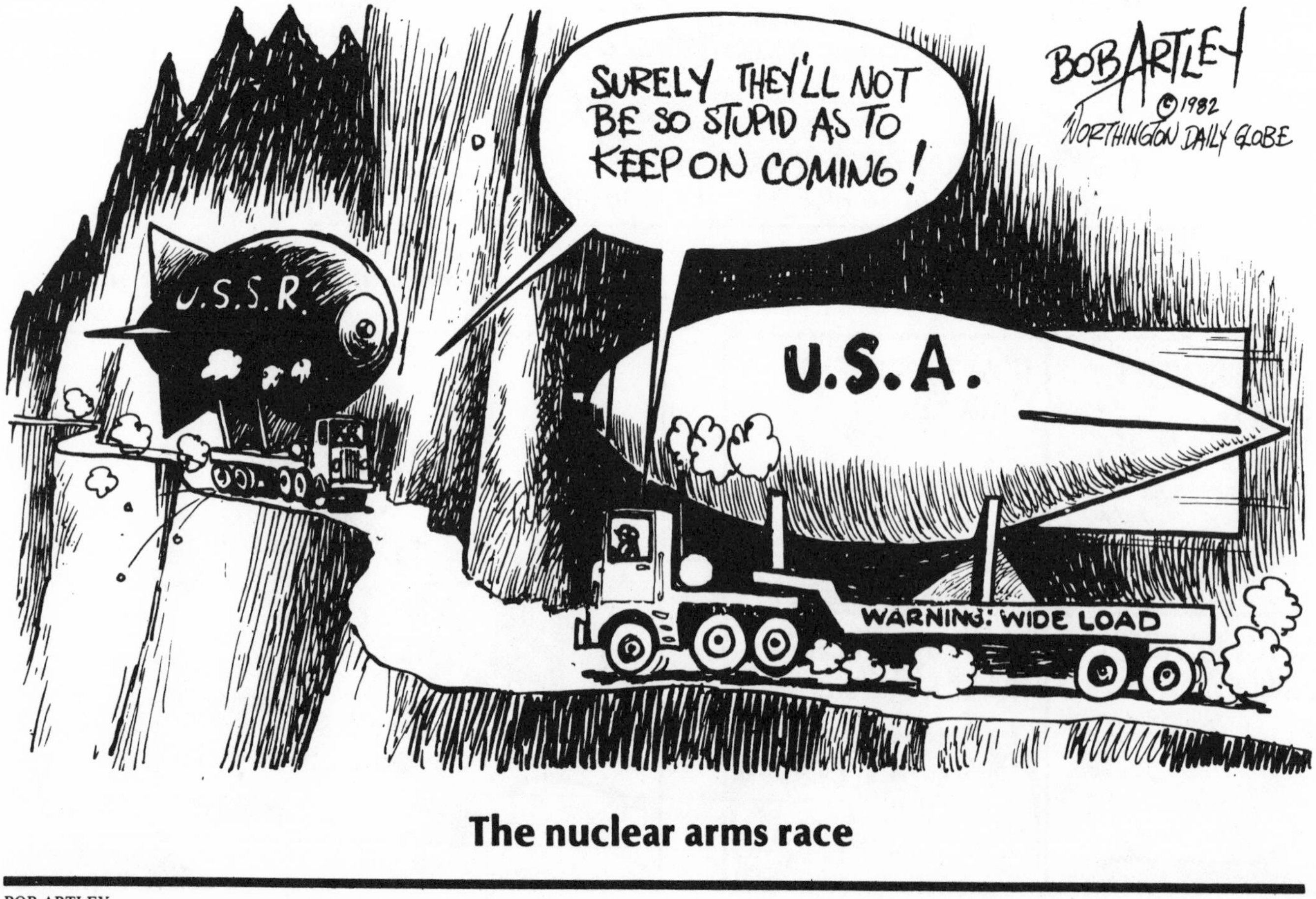
SURELY THEY'LL NOT BE SO STUPID AS TO KEEP ON COMING!
BOB ARTLEY ©1982 WORTHINGTON DAILY GLOBE
U.S.S.R.
U.S.A.
WARNING: WIDE LOAD

The nuclear arms race

BOB ARTLEY
Courtesy Worthington (Minn.) Daily Globe

STEVE GREENBERG
Courtesy Los Angeles Daily News

JOHN BRANCH
Courtesy San Antonio Express–News

BILL SANDERS
Courtesy Milwaukee Journal

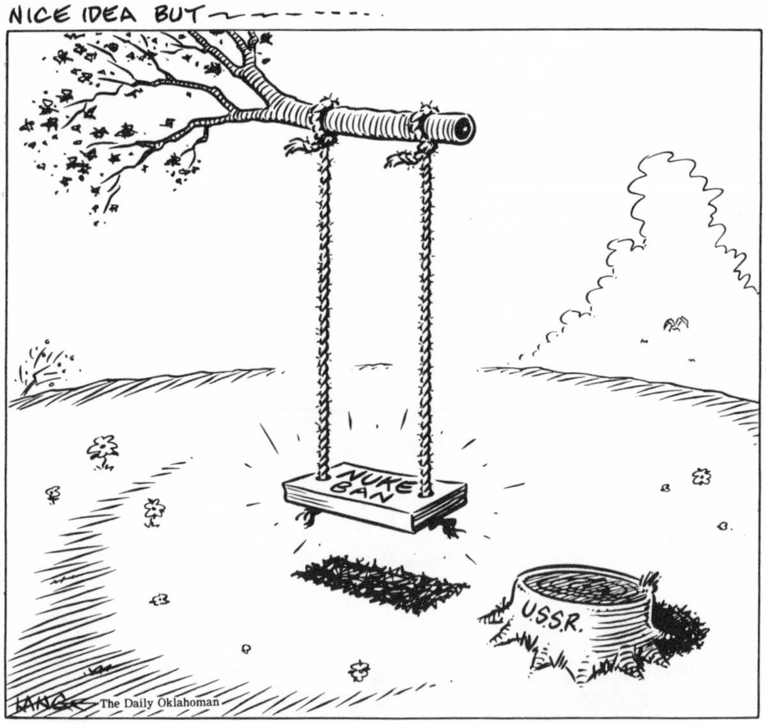
NICE IDEA BUT
NUKE BAN
U.S.S.R.
LANGE The Daily Oklahoman

JIM LANGE
Courtesy Daily Oklahoman

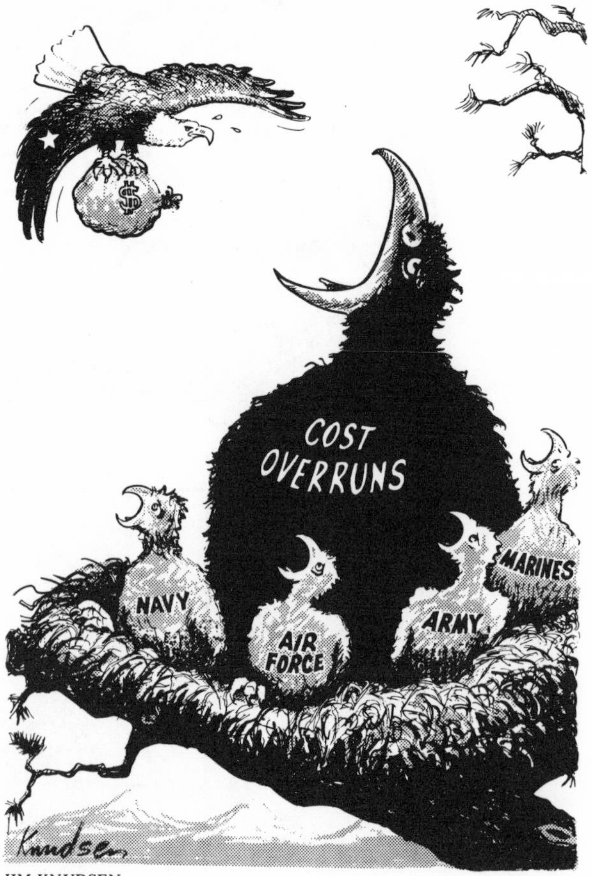
$
COST OVERRUNS
NAVY
AIR FORCE
ARMY
MARINES
Knudsen

JIM KNUDSEN
Courtesy L.A. Tidings

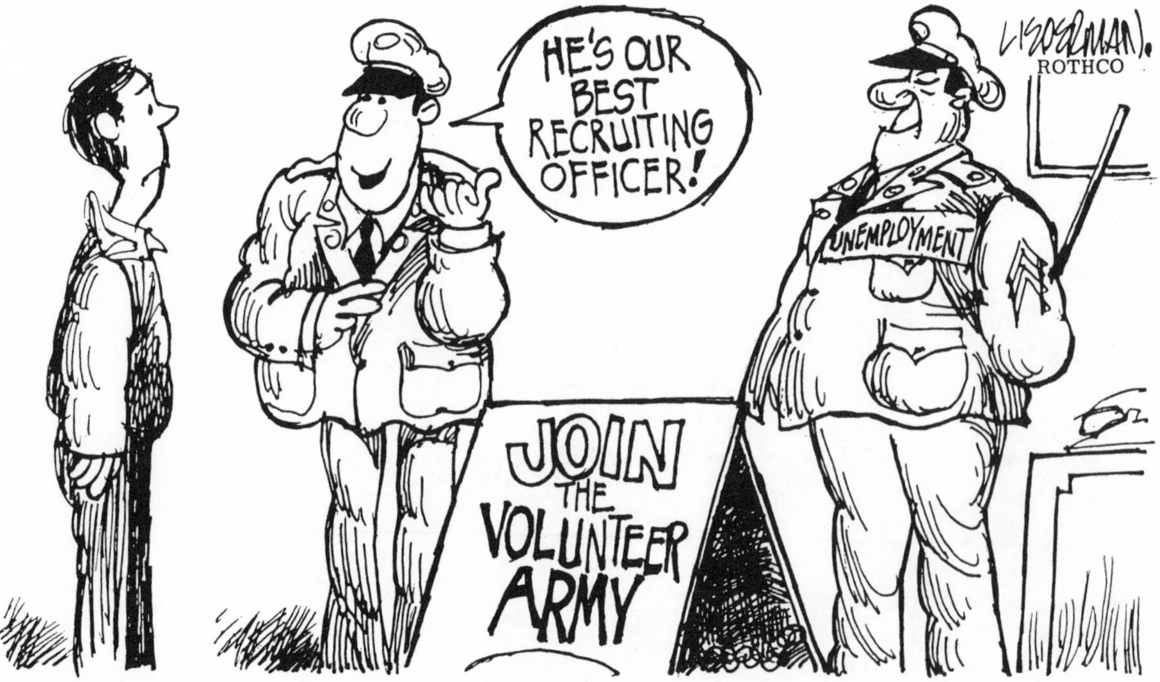
HE'S OUR BEST RECRUITING OFFICER!
ROTHCO
UNEMPLOYMENT
JOIN THE VOLUNTEER ARMY

AL LIEDERMAN
©Rothco

The Economy

The 1981 recession continued throughout 1982—and was the worst since the 1930s. Unemployment soared to the highest levels since World War II, with more than 10 percent of the labor force out of work. More businesses went bankrupt than at any time since the Great Depression, and farm income plummeted. Several banks failed, along with scores of savings and loan institutions; high interest rates slowed sales and profits.

By late summer interest rates had fallen significantly, with the prime rate dropping from 16.5 percent to 12 percent. By year's end inflation had been brought under control, showing a 1982 rate of only 3.9 percent, the lowest one-year rise in a decade.

Airlines faced rough flying during the year, with Braniff, one of the oldest airlines in the U.S., declaring bankruptcy. The automobile industry had its worst year since 1961 as imports captured 29.2 percent of total sales. Although sales were down, the industry showed modest profits through a variety of cost-cutting measures.

BILL SANDERS
Courtesy Milwaukee Journal

DAVID SATTLER
*Courtesy Lafayette (Ind.) Journal and
Courier*

BRUCE BEATTIE
*Courtesy Daytona Beach
News–Journal*

JIM LARRICK
Courtesy Columbus Dispatch

"You eat your SUSHI! Think of the starving American
auto workers who would just love to have your food"

KEN ALEXANDER
Courtesy San Francisco Examiner

DICK LOCHER
Courtesy Chicago Tribune

BOB ZSCHIESCHE
©Zschiesche Cartoons

WALT HANDELSMAN
Courtesy Catonville Times

50

The Exorci$t

HUGH HAYNIE
Courtesy Louisville Courier–Journal

JIM BERRY
©NEA

"This one is either 'Unemployment' or 'Herpes.' I don't have my glasses."

EDD ULUSCHAK
Courtesy Edmonton Journal

"Good news — I got a month's advance. The bad news is they called it 'severance pay!'"

BRUCE PLANTE
Courtesy Fayetteville Times (N.C.)

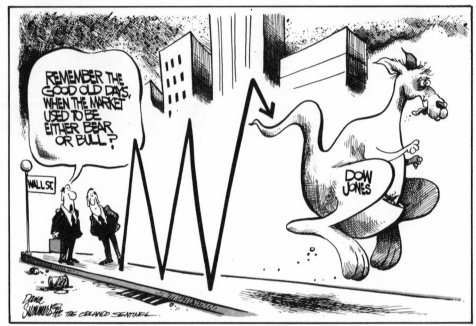

DANA SUMMERS
Courtesy The Sentinel

KATE SALLEY PALMER
Courtesy Greenville News

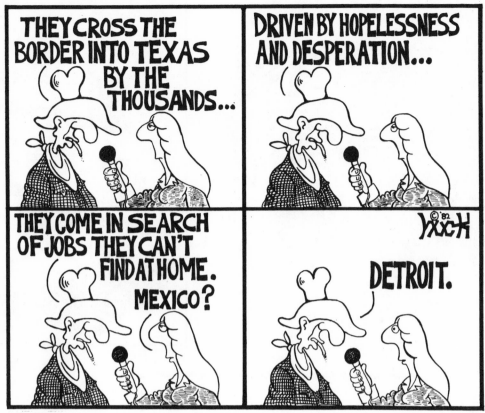

GARY HUCK
Courtesy Racine Labor

WAYNE STAYSKAL
Courtesy Chicago Tribune

"Of Course, We Can't Blame Everything on Foreign Imports"

TOM FLANNERY
Courtesy Baltimore Sun

CLYDE PETERSON
Courtesy Houston Chronicle

RICHARD ALLISON
Courtesy Army Times

JOHN BRANCH
Courtesy San Antonio Express–News

KARL HUBENTHAL
Courtesy Los Angeles Herald–Examiner

DOUG MACGREGOR
Courtesy Norwich Bulletin

BOUNTIFUL HARVEST

JERRY BARNETT
Courtesy Indianapolis News

ROBERT SULLIVAN
Courtesy Worcester Telegram

DICK LOCHER
Courtesy Chicago Tribune

JIM MORGAN
Courtesy Spartanburg Herald–Journal

'THE RECESSION WILL SOON BOTTOM-OUT'

BRUCE BEATTIE
*Courtesy Daytona Beach
News–Journal*

"Luggage isn't the only thing we've been losing
a lot of lately... See any profits in there?"

JACK BENDER
Courtesy Waterloo Courier

DICK WALLMEYER
Courtesy Independent Press–Telegram
(Calif.)

ED ASHLEY
Courtesy Toledo Blade

Foreign Affairs

Throughout 1982 China continued to demand that the U.S. cut off arms sales to Taiwan. During visits by Vice-President George Bush and Sen. Howard Baker, the Chinese pressed for repeal of the Taiwan Relations Act of 1979 that committed the U.S. to the safeguarding of Taiwan's security. The U.S. promised not to increase arms sales to Taiwan and declared its intention to reduce sales over an unspecified time.

In Northern Ireland the two major Unionist parties won 47 seats in the 78-seat assembly, while the radical Catholic Sinn Fein scored better than expected, capturing five seats. A series of terrorist acts followed the elections. In June an economic summit conference of the world's seven major noncommunist industrial countries was held in France at the palace of Versailles. President Reagan took part in the meeting.

In October Swedish naval forces detected what they suspected was a Soviet submarine close to their coastline near a secret naval base. After several days of fruitless searching, the Swedish navy assumed the submarine had escaped to the open sea.

A CIA estimate that Pakistan could develop the ability to explode a nuclear device within three years raised worldwide concern, but President Zia pledged that the country would not develop such a weapon.

TOM CURTIS
Courtesy Milwaukee Sentinel

Sweet and sour pork

KEN ALEXANDER
Courtesy San Francisco Examiner

KEVIN KALLAUGHER
©K.K. Syndication Service (Eng.)

THE ONLY MURDER
FOR WHICH BOTH THE IRA AND PROTESTANTS
CAN CLAIM RESPOSIBILITY.

BILL DE ORE
Courtesy Dallas Morning News

FRANK EVERS
Courtesy New York Daily News

ETTA HULME
Courtesy Ft. Worth Star–Telegram

DANA SUMMERS
Courtesy The Sentinel

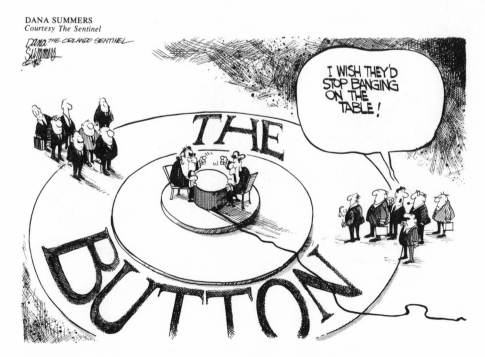

JACK JURDEN
*Courtesy Wilmington Evening
Journal–News*

JOHN COLLINS
Courtesy Montreal Gazette

MERLE TINGLEY
Courtesy London Free Press (Can.)

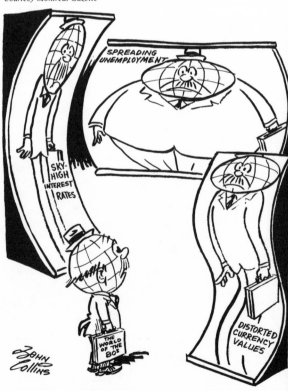

VERSAILLES: THE HALL of MIRRORS

Law and the Courts

The question of prayer in the schools continued to be a political issue in 1982. On May 6 President Reagan announced he would support a constitutional amendment that would allow voluntary prayer in public schools. Supreme Court rulings have prohibited school prayer, but an amendment would supersede the rulings.

Sen. Jesse Helms introduced legislation to deny the federal courts jurisdiction over the prayer issue, but the measure was defeated in the Senate. Polls indicate that Reagan's proposed amendment has strong public support, but advocates agreed that ratification would be a long, hard process.

John W. Hinckley Jr. was found not guilty by reason of insanity of the shooting of President Reagan and three others in 1981. America was outraged by the verdict, and calls for restrictions on the insanity defense were heard from all sides. Many citizens seemed to support the elimination of the insanity plea as a defense.

LARRY WRIGHT
Courtesy Detroit News

DAVID SATTLER
Courtesy Lafayette (Ind.) Journal and Courier

TIM MENEES
Courtesy Pittsburgh Post–Gazette

VIC RUNTZ
Courtesy Bangor Daily News

KATE SALLEY PALMER
Courtesy Greenville News

Schools have prayer time already

64

JACK MCLEOD
Courtesy Buffalo Evening News

BOB TAYLOR
Courtesy Dallas Times-Herald

JERRY ROBINSON
©Cartoonists & Writers Syndicate

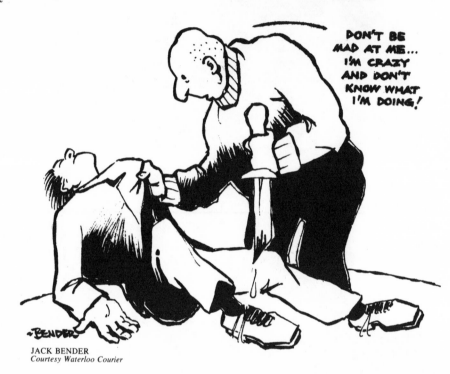

JACK BENDER
Courtesy Waterloo Courier

MIKE MORGAN
Courtesy Macon Telegraph & News

EUGENE PAYNE
Courtesy Charlotte Observer

DRAPER HILL
Courtesy Detroit News

CHUCK BROOKS
Courtesy Birmingham News

JERRY DOYLE
Courtesy Philadelphia Daily News

JERRY BARNETT
Courtesy Indianapolis News

The Democrats

Prospects for the Democrats brightened in 1982 as the party gained 26 seats in the House of Representatives and seven governorships while breaking even in Senate elections. Pollster Louis Harris called the elections "a decisive defeat" for the New Right. Few of the winning Democrats, however, could be classified as big-spending liberals. Nevertheless the election seemed to send President Reagan a warning to steer a more moderate course.

In Alabama Republican Emory Folmar was defeated by a rejuvenated George Wallace. Wallace won with strong black support, despite his well-known segregationist stand in the past.

Although the Democrats picked up strength in the House, pollsters pointed out that the public felt Democrats had failed to offer viable alternatives to Reagan's plan.

On December 1 Sen. Ted Kennedy announced that he would not be a candidate for president in 1984, thus producing a scramble among would-be Democratic candidates.

A survey showed that a majority of television newscasters lean toward the Democratic Party. Conservatives have complained for years about slanted television reporting, but the networks responded by once again denying any bias.

JON KENNEDY
Courtesy Arkansas Democrat

Democrats' dilemna...

PHIL BISSELL
Courtesy Lowell (Mass.) Sun

KARL HUBENTHAL
Courtesy Los Angeles Herald–Examiner

DICK LOCHER
Courtesy Chicago Tribune

JOHN LARTER
Courtesy Toronto Star

ED GAMBLE
Courtesy Florida Times–Union

ASTRONOMERS FIND HUGE HOLE IN SPACE, ABSOLUTELY NOTHING THERE.

JIM DOBBINS
Courtesy Union–Leader

GEORGE FISHER
Courtesy Arkansas Gazette

JIM PALMER
Courtesy Montgomery Advertiser

The Middle East

In June Israel launched a massive invasion of Lebanon in an attempt to clear all Palestine Liberation Organization and Syrian forces from the country. Overpowered by Israeli armed might, the PLO finally began withdrawing in August to new locations in eight Arab nations. The invasion left many scars, and Israel's relations with the U.S. and Western Europe were severely strained.

Hundreds of Palestinian men, women, and children were massacred in two refugee camps by Phalangist militiamen after the PLO withdrawal. They had been allowed to enter the camps by Israeli troops ostensibly to clear out any remaining PLO forces. An investigation was launched to determine whether the government of Prime Minister Menachem Begin was directly responsible for the murders.

On April 25 Israel withdrew from the Sinai, an area they had captured from Egypt during the 1967 war. They refused to give up control of the West Bank, however, and implemented a new occupation policy. Mayors in the area were fired if they refused to deal with the new Israeli military administrator.

A growing world oil glut forced crude oil production to decline 7.4 percent below the 1981 level.

BILL GARNER
Courtesy Commercial Appeal (Memphis)

ELDON PLETCHER
Courtesy New Orleans Times–Picayune

DICK LOCHER
Courtesy Chicago Tribune

"IT'S NOT ISRAEL'S RIGHT TO EXIST THAT CONCERNS ME RIGHT NOW!"

PAUL SZEP
Courtesy Boston Globe

REAGAN, BEGIN AND NOD

DENNIS RENAULT
Courtesy Sacramento Bee

The American Falcon

FRANK EVERS
Courtesy New York Daily News

TOM CURTIS
Courtesy Milwaukee Sentinel

"It must have happened when I wasn't looking!"

ROGER HARVELL
Courtesy Pine Bluff Commercial

JACK OHMAN
Courtesy Detroit Free Press

ROB LAWLOR
Courtesy Philadelphia Daily News

PAUL CONRAD
Courtesy Los Angeles Times

ROY PETERSON
Courtesy Vancouver Sun

"I'm sorry, Mr. Reagan . . . Mr. Begin just stepped out . . ."

ED FISCHER
Courtesy Rochester Post–Bulletin

'YOU KNOW THE OLD SAYING – WOMEN AND
CHILDREN FIRST...'

JOSEPH HELLER
Courtesy West Bend News (Wisc.)

"THERE WILL NEVER BE ANOTHER HOLOCAUST" – MENACHEM BEGIN.

TERRY MOSHER (AISLIN)
Courtesy Montreal Gazette

GEORGE FISHER
Courtesy Arkansas Gazette

ED STEIN
Courtesy Rocky Mountain News

MIKE JENKINS
Courtesy Beaumont Enterprise

There's no bottom to it

BOB ARTLEY
Courtesy Worthington (Minn.)
Daily Globe

CHUCK ASAY
Courtesy Colorado Springs Sun

BOB GORRELL
Courtesy Charlotte News

No me Defiendas, Compadre

LUIS BORJA
Courtesy Caricatura Nacional

EDGAR SOLLER
Courtesy Fil–American News

CHAN LOWE
Courtesy Oklahoma City Times

DWANE POWELL
Courtesy News & Observer (N.C.)
© 1982 The News and Observer—Los Angeles Times Syndicate

EUGENE PAYNE
Courtesy Charlotte Observer

Lebanon war

world opinion war

DICK WRIGHT
Courtesy Providence (R.I.)
Journal—Bulletin

CHARLES DANIEL
Courtesy Knoxville Journal

CRAIG MACINTOSH
Courtesy Minneapolis Star–Tribune

ROB LAWLOR
Courtesy Philadelphia Daily News

MIKE GRASTON
Courtesy Windsor Star (Ont.)

HELPING ISRAEL OUT

JIM DOBBINS
Courtesy Union-Leader

EDGAR SOLLER
Courtesy Fil-American News

CRACKING UP

KARL HUBENTHAL
Courtesy Los Angeles Herald–Examiner

Poland

Imposed in late 1981, martial law failed to restore social peace to the country. The U.S. had immediately suspended all economic aid, banned the Polish airline and fishing fleet from U.S. territory, and also restricted Polish diplomats in their movements in the U.S.

On May Day about 30,000 Poles took to the streets demanding that Lech Walesa, leader of the banned Solidarity labor union, be released from prison. Bitter clashes took place between defiant Solidarity supporters and police, resulting in scores of injured and more than 1,000 arrests.

In response to a call from Solidarity to mark the second anniversary of its creation, tens of thousands of Polish citizens gathered in cities across the country. General Wojciech Jaruzelski, premier and communist party chairman, sought to gain public support for the military regime, but did not succeed.

Late in the year the government announced the release of Walesa and other labor leaders, but their freedom seemed to be in name only.

DAVID HORSEY
Courtesy Seattle Post–Intelligencer

MARGULIES

JIMMY MARGULIES
© Rothco

ED GAMBLE
Courtesy Florida Times–Union

BILL GARNER
Courtesy Commercial Appeal (Memphis)

POLISH MARTIAL LAW 1982

HUGH HAYNIE
Courtesy Louisville Courier-Journal

'Don't give me that bends but won't break stuff — hit it again!'

CHUCK AYERS
Courtesy Akron Beacon–Journal

V. CULLUM ROGERS
Courtesy Durham Morning Herald

BEN SARGENT
Courtesy Austin American–Statesman

CLIFF BALDOWSKI
Courtesy Atlanta Constitution

"... ME? I'M THE BABYSITTER!...WHO'RE YOU?"

Latin America

On July 4 Miguel de la Madrid Hurtado was named president of Mexico. His predecessor, Jose Lopez Portillo, had begun a massive modernization program that required borrowing vast sums of money after rich oil deposits were discovered in the early 1970s. The decline in oil prices threw the nation's economy into a shambles, and the country teetered on the brink of bankruptcy. Banks were nationalized and currency controls were imposed. By summer the nation's debt to foreign creditors had risen to $80 billion. Adding to Mexico's woes was the eruption of the Chichonal volcano in March that killed nearly 200 and left thousands homeless.

War-torn El Salvador held a free election, and, although rebels threatened to kill anyone who voted, more than 1.5 million ballots were cast. The centrist Christian Democrats failed to win a majority, and rightist Roberto d'Aubuisson formed a coalition to rule the 60-member assembly.

Late in the year President Reagan traveled to Central America, visiting several nations and stressing the need for increased trade and investment and closer ties with the United States.

H. CLAY BENNETT
Courtesy St. Petersburg Times

"Quick! Blame the bankers!"

Trabajo, sí, Pero...
"Work, yes, but . . ."

—¿Tienes cartas de recomendación?
"Do you have letters of recommendation?"

LUIS BORJA
Courtesy Caricatura Nacional

OLLIE HARRINGTON
Courtesy N.Y. Daily World

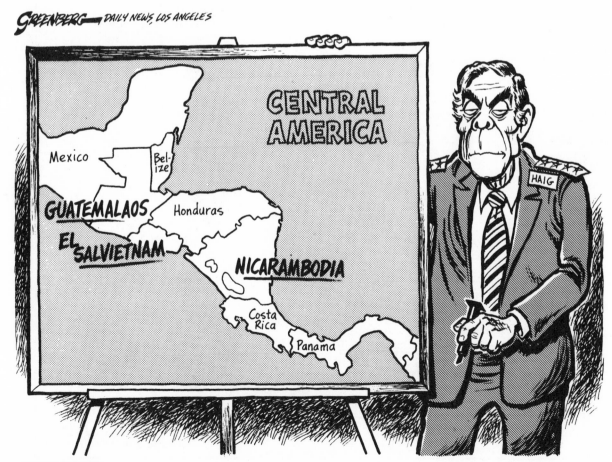

STEVE GREENBERG
Courtesy Los Angeles Daily News

JOHN LARTER
Courtesy Toronto Star

PAUL SZEP
Courtesy Boston Globe

JIM BERRY
©NEA

©1982 by NEA, Inc

"Has Argentina given you any ideas about the U.S. base on Guantanamo Bay?"

TOM ENGELHARDT
Courtesy St. Louis Post-Dispatch

'It's A Re-Make Of A '60s Movie That Starred Lyndon Johnson'

DAVID HORSEY
Courtesy Seattle Post-Intelligencer

LAZARO FRESQUET
Courtesy El Miami Herald

ART BIMROSE
Courtesy The Oregonian

V. CULLUM ROGERS
Courtesy Durham Morning Herald

Great Britain

War broke out in March when Argentina invaded the Falkland Islands, virtually daring Great Britain to respond. The British did respond and, when the war ended ten weeks later, the British flag prevailed—more than 1,000 troops had been killed, and billions had been spent.

The mini-war between two limited combatants gave a chilling preview of what a conventional war with modern high technology could be like. The question was raised, for example, that if a $50 million destroyer such as Britain's *Sheffield* could be destroyed by a $200,000 Argentine missile, could not such a weapon also devastate a $1 billion U.S. fleet defense cruiser? Experts began to worry that big ships might be too vulnerable to today's highly sophisticated missiles.

On June 21 Princess Diana gave birth to a boy, who was christened William Arthur Philip Louis and is second in line to the British throne.

In July Britain was outraged when an intruder, Michael Fagan, successfully breached security and made his way to the queen's bedroom. The queen chatted with the interloper before calling security guards.

BOB ENGLEHART
Courtesy Hartford Courant

DAVID WILEY MILLER
©Copley News Service

The Louse that Roared

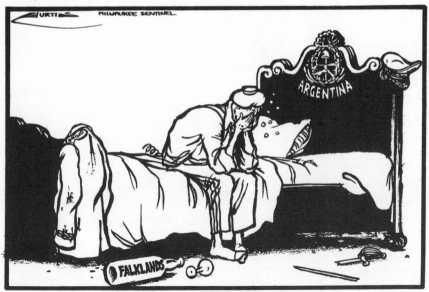

The morning after

THE L. A. TIMES SYNDICATE

We're steaming toward
the Falklands,
With a fervent vow
to win!
Just get me outa this
bloody stew,
And I'll explain how
I got in.

HUGH HAYNIE
Courtesy Louisville Courier–Journal

DARCY

The Iron Lady.

TOM DARCY
Courtesy Newsday

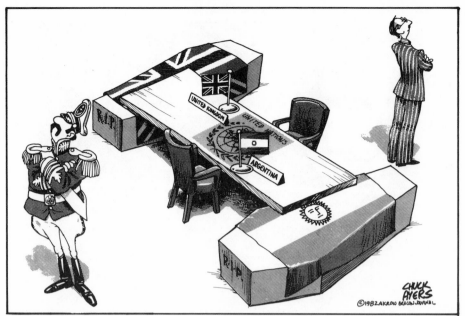

CHUCK AYERS
Courtesy Akron Beacon-Journal

"...MUST BE SAILING UNDER NEW MARKINGS!"

CLIFF BALDOWSKI
Courtesy Atlanta Constitution

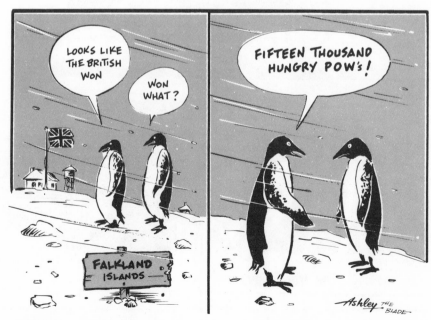

ED ASHLEY
Courtesy Toledo Blade

'Ah, Yes, If You'll Turn Your Attention to our Seizure of the Falkland Islands'

CRAIG MACINTOSH
Courtesy Minneapolis Star–Tribune

MIKE JENKINS
Courtesy Beaumont Enterprise

TERRY MOSHER (AISLIN)
Courtesy Montreal Gazette

BEN SARGENT
Courtesy Austin American–Statesman

DICK WALLMEYER
Courtesy Independent Press–Telegram
(Calif.)

DRAPER HILL
Courtesy Detroit News

BILL GARNER
Courtesy Commercial Appeal (Memphis)

V. CULLUM ROGERS
Courtesy Durham Morning Herald

...I see
The imminent death of twenty thousand men,
That for a fancy and a trick of fame
Go to their graves like beds, fight for a plot
Whereon the numbers cannot try the cause,
Which is not tomb enough and continent
To hide the slain....

— Hamlet

PAUL SZEP
Courtesy Boston Globe

BRITISH ACE

ROB LAWLOR
Courtesy Philadelphia Daily News

MERLE TINGLEY
Courtesy London Free Press (Can.)

104

MIKE GRASTON
Courtesy Windsor Star (Ont.)

CHUCK BROOKS
Courtesy Birmingham News

BRIAN GABLE
Courtesy Regina Leader–Post (Sask.)

TOM MEYER
Courtesy San Francisco Chronicle

VERN THOMPSON
Courtesy Lawton (Okla.) Constitution

MIKE PETERS
Courtesy Dayton Daily News

James Watt and the Environment

The policies of Secretary of the Interior James G. Watt continued to be the center of controversy during the year. Brickbats were thrown at him regularly by environmentalist groups because of his stand on the sale and leasing of federal lands.

The secretary believes that America should be aware of oil deposits and valuable minerals on government-owned land in case of a world-wide conflict. He does not favor acquiring additional land for national parks, contending that present parks should be modernized and repaired first.

Environmentalists berated Watt for opening large areas of the outer continental shelf for oil and gas leasing. The Department of the Interior has leased over 4 million acres of the total one billion shelf acres. These leases have produced $17.5 billion in badly needed revenue.

Since the federal government owns about one-third of the land in the continental U.S., Secretary Watt maintains that a confrontation with Russia over oil in the Middle East might be averted if America is aware of all its oil and mineral reserves in advance.

EDGAR SOLLER
Courtesy Fil–American News

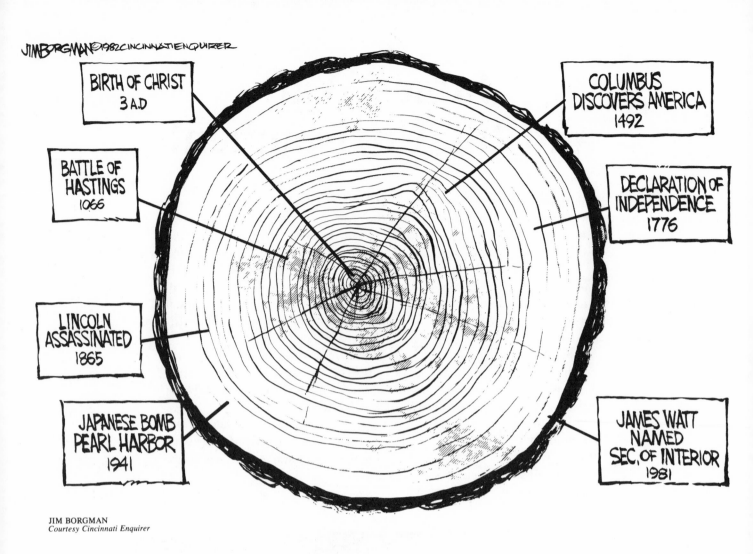

BIRTH OF CHRIST
3 A.D

BATTLE OF
HASTINGS
1066

COLUMBUS
DISCOVERS AMERICA
1492

DECLARATION OF
INDEPENDENCE
1776

LINCOLN
ASSASSINATED
1865

JAPANESE BOMB
PEARL HARBOR
1941

JAMES WATT
NAMED
SEC. OF INTERIOR
1981

JIM BORGMAN
Courtesy Cincinnati Enquirer

WATT
OIL CO.

MIKE MORGAN
Courtesy Macon Telegraph & News

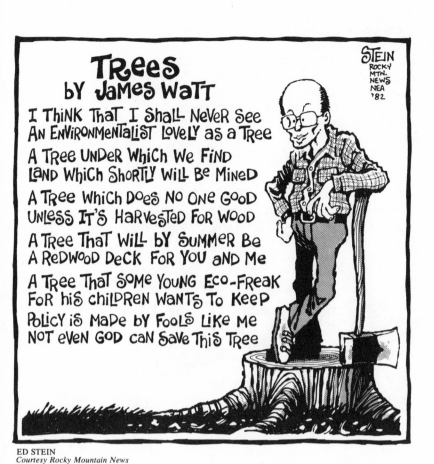

Trees
by James Watt

STEIN
ROCKY
MTN.
NEWS
NEA
'82

I Think That I Shall Never See
An Environmentalist Lovely as a Tree

A Tree Under Which We Find
Land Which Shortly Will Be Mined

A Tree Which Does No One Good
Unless It's Harvested For Wood

A Tree That Will by Summer Be
A Redwood Deck For You and Me

A Tree That Some Young Eco-Freak
For His Children Wants To Keep

Policy Is Made by Fools Like Me
Not Even God Can Save This Tree

ED STEIN
Courtesy Rocky Mountain News

ALL-OUT
OFFSHORE
DRILLING

WATT

OIL
COMPANIES

ENGELHARDT
©1982 St. Louis Post-Dispatch

'Last One In Is A National Security Risk!'

Trees

Poems are made
by fools like me.
But only God can
make a tree.
J.K.

SO WATT?

OIL LEASES FOR
90 MILLION
SCENIC CALIFORNIA
COAST ACRES

Bissell

CHARLES BISSELL
Courtesy The Tennessean

GEORGE FISHER
Courtesy Arkansas Gazette

BOB ENGLEHART
Courtesy Hartford Courant

JERRY FEARING
Courtesy St. Paul Dispatch–
Pioneer Press

JERRY ROBINSON
©Cartoonists & Writers Syndicate

WATT MAN

AND WATT SAID, 'LET THERE BE BALDNESS, IN MY OWN IMAGE AND LIKENESS.' AND IT WAS SO.

CLIFF BALDOWSKI
Courtesy Atlanta Constitution

"...ENVIRONMENTAL PROTECTION AGENCY!...OH, HELLO, MR. PRESIDENT!
...YES SIR, FOLLOWING YOUR DIRECTIONS TO THE LETTER...WORKING
WELL WITHIN OUR BUDGET..."

CHARLES BISSELL
Courtesy The Tennessean

Wanderer For The Wasteland

BRUCE PLANTE
Courtesy Fayetteville Times (N.C.)

JOHN COLLINS
Courtesy Montreal Gazette

WAYNE STAYSKAL
Courtesy Chicago Tribune

114

Crime

In late September and early October seven persons died after taking cyanide-laced Extra-Strength Tylenol capsules purchased over the counter in the Chicago area. The manufacturer immediately recalled all Tylenol capsules.

Authorities believed that an individual, possibly a disgruntled employee or an extortionist, committed the terrible deed. A massive investigation was launched, involving both federal and state agents, but at year's end no one had been charged with the crime.

Halloween was a much more subdued occasion than usual because of the Tylenol murders and other instances of poisons showing up in candy and other packaged foods across the country.

Crime in major cities across the U.S. continued to rise during the year. Even rural crime registered an increase.

A verdict of not guilty by reason of insanity in the trial of John W. Hinckley Jr. set off a barrage of public protest. The 27-year-old drifter was sent to a mental hospital after the jury decided he was not responsible for his actions when he shot President Reagan and three others.

CORKY
Courtesy Honolulu Star–Bulletin

CHARLES DANIEL
Courtesy Knoxville Journal

CHUCK ASAY
Courtesy Colorado Springs Sun

WAYNE STAYSKAL
Courtesy Chicago Tribune

" I EVEN CHECK CIGARETTE PACKAGES NOW-A-DAYS (COUGH, COUGH) JUST TO
MAKE SURE (HACK, WHEEZE) NOBODY'S POISONING ME ! "

LARRY WRIGHT
Courtesy Detroit News

JOHN CRAWFORD
Courtesy Alabama Journal

"DON'T EAT ANY OF THOSE GOODIES UNTIL THEY'VE BEEN CHECKED"

DANA SUMMERS
Courtesy The Sentinel

JIM PALMER
Courtesy Montgomery Advertiser

KIRK WALTERS
Courtesy Scranton Times

BOB BECKETT
Courtesy New Jersey
Newspapers Service

TOM DARCY
Courtesy Newsday

118

PHIL BISSELL
Courtesy Lowell (Mass.) Sun

DOUBLE BARRELED TROUBLE ON A DOUBLE BARRELED HIGHWAY

BRIAN BASSET
Courtesy Seattle Times

The Soviet Union

In 1982 the leadership in Moscow seemed content to avoid making waves. Communist Party General Secretary Leonid Brezhnev had been in failing health for many months, and on November 10 he died of a heart attack. Two days later the Central Committee selected as his replacement Yuri Andropov, who had served as chairman of the Soviet security police and foreign intelligence agency (KGB).

An estimated 100,000 Russian troops remained bogged down in Afghanistan. The Afghan tribesmen proved to be fierce fighters, and there appeared little likelihood of any conclusion to the war in the near future.

For the fourth consecutive year Russia was unable to feed its people without large-scale outside aid. The U.S.S.R. is expected to buy more than 8 million tons of grain from the U.S. in 1983.

Evangelist Billy Graham visited Russia for the first time following an invitation by the head of the Russian Orthodox Church. Graham's visit stirred criticism in the U.S. and among Russian Protestants, who claimed he had not spoken out on the lack of religious freedom in the country.

Evidence was presented during the year proving that the Soviet Union has used chemical and toxic weapons in Laos, Cambodia, and Afghanistan.

H. CLAY BENNETT
Courtesy St. Petersburg Times

"SEE ? AND THE SLIMY AFGHANS DO THE SAME THING TO OUR HELICOPTER BLADES AND ARTILLERY !"

CHUCK BROOKS
Courtesy Birmingham News

BILL DE ORE
Courtesy Dallas Morning News

PAUL SZEP
Courtesy Boston Globe

NEWS ITEM: BREZHNEV TRIES RECONCILIATION WITH CHINA

ELDON PLETCHER
Courtesy New Orleans Times–Picayune

The Times-Picayune
The States-Item
PLETCHER

JOHN TREVER
Courtesy Albuquerque Journal

ETTA HULME
Courtesy Ft. Worth Star–Telegram

"IF Y'ALL ARE EVAH NEAH MONTREAT, N.C., Y'ALL DROP BY, HEAH?"

JACK OHMAN
Courtesy Detroit Free Press

BRIAN GABLE
Courtesy Regina Leader–Post (Sask.)

'. . . Sometimes I'm Astounded at the Incredible Advance in Technology That I've Witnessed in my LIFETIME!

VIC CANTONE
© Rothco

'And we'd be happy to restore peace in the Mideast, too.'

TOM DARCY
Courtesy Newsday

Pro Football Strike

For eight long mid-season weeks professional football fans had to look elsewhere for entertainment as National Football League players went out on strike September 21. It was the first regular-season strike in the 63-year history of the league.

Ed Garvey, chief bargainer for the players, initially sought a contract calling for players to receive 55 percent of the gross income of each team, which would have just about doubled every player's salary. Management balked and refused to agree to any fixed percentage. Under mounting pressure a tentative five-year pact was reached on November 16. Under the new agreement salaries were increased from a $30,000 minimum for rookies to a $200,000 minimum for an 18-year player. The strike cut the regular 16-game season to 9 games, and 16 teams, instead of the usual 10, competed in the playoffs for the Super Bowl.

Evidence of widespread use of cocaine by players also became public in 1982. One drug consultant estimated that about 40 percent of the players use cocaine at one time or another and that 15 percent are "problem users."

DWANE POWELL
Courtesy News & Observer (N.C.)

MIKE PETERS
Courtesy Dayton Daily News

PSST... THINK THERE'S ANYTHING TO THIS NFL DRUG BUSINESS..?

 ART HENRIKSON
© Paddock Publications

ELDON PLETCHER
Courtesy New Orleans Times–Picayune

JIM LANGE
Courtesy Daily Oklahoman

RAY OSRIN
Courtesy Cleveland Plain Dealer

LARRY WRIGHT
Courtesy Detroit News

127

THE POOR FANS

JACK JURDEN
*Courtesy Wilmington Evening
Journal–News*

JIMMY MARGULIES
© Rothco

MIKE KEEFE
Courtesy Denver Post

128

Canadian Politics

Canada suffered its worst economic slump since the Great Depression as unemployment rose to 12 percent in September. Inflation also plagued the economy, hovering around 10 percent for the year. Many companies went bankrupt, and others were forced to implement major economizing measures to survive.

The mining industry laid off 70,000 of its 130,000 workers by midyear, and there were heavy personnel cutbacks in automobile factories, farm machinery plants, and most areas of manufacturing. The west coast forest industry was especially hard hit.

Bitter constitutional controversies continued to preoccupy Prime Minister Pierre Elliott Trudeau's attention until the country's basic law was brought under Canadian control on April 17. The Constitution Act, signed as Queen Elizabeth II looked on, gave Canada the power to amend its own constitution—a right Britain had retained after granting independence to Canada.

Late in the year auto workers struck the Chrysler plant, pushing the automobile giant close to insolvency.

EDD ULUSCHAK
Courtesy Edmonton Journal

"I'm sure the autopsy should tell us more about your condition."

ADRIAN RAESIDE
Courtesy Times—Colonist (B.C.)

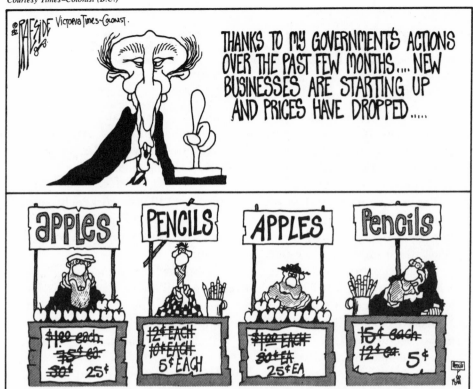

ROY PETERSON
Courtesy Vancouver Sun

"I keep telling you — it's a deep recession not a depression . . . now eat your Alpo . . ."

". . . patience Igor, we keep creating them until we get it right . . ."

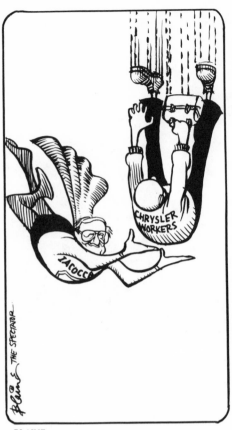

BLAINE
Courtesy The Spectator (Ont.)

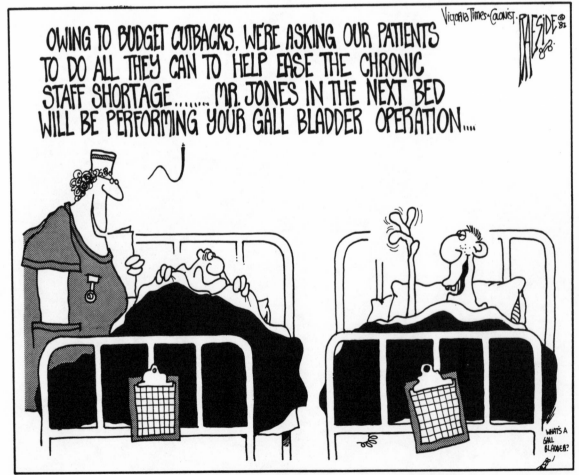

ADRIAN RAESIDE
Courtesy Times–Colonist (B.C.)

BRIAN GABLE
Courtesy Regina Leader–Post (Sask.)

MIKE GRASTON
Courtesy Windsor Star (Ont.)

JOHN COLLINS
Courtesy Montreal Gazette

HIS MASTERS' VOICES

Social Security

During the year President Reagan offered a proposal to take Social Security out of politics and turn the problem over to a bipartisan study panel. The National Commission on Social Security Reform included members appointed by the president and by Senate Majority Leader Howard Baker and House Speaker Tip O'Neill.

The Senate budget committee proposed that the Social Security trust funds be increased by $40 billion over fiscal 1983-85 to keep the system solvent. This could be achieved by increasing payroll taxes or through benefit cuts. The idea aroused much consternation, and it was quickly dropped. One thing remained certain, however: Something has to be done, or the Social Security system will go bankrupt.

Robert J. Myers, the commission's executive director, says the problem is caused by the fact that prices have risen much faster than wages during the past five years. And prices, through the Consumer Price Index, determine Social Security cost-of-living adjustments.

JERRY BARNETT
Courtesy Indianapolis News

CHARLES KELLER
Courtesy N.Y. Daily World

JON KENNEDY
Courtesy Arkansas Democrat

REAGAN: *"Welcome to my supply side, across-the-board, trickle-down, budget-balancing program!"*

Quick-change artist

FRANK EVERS
Courtesy New York Daily News

DRAPER HILL
Courtesy Detroit News

Soviet Pipeline

The Soviet pipeline that will bring Siberian natural gas to Europe caused strained relations between the U.S. and its European allies. After the Senate had cracked down on Poland, President Reagan barred U.S. firms from selling equipment needed for the construction of the 3,000 mile pipeline.

European allies were infuriated when the ban was extended to foreign subsidiaries of American firms and to foreign companies making the equipment under American licenses. The pipeline was being financed with Western European credits in return for future gas deliveries.

On August 26 a French company loaded three 60-ton compressors on a freighter bound for Russia. The French government had directly ordered the company to proceed with the shipments. When Reagan realized that American allies would not support his ban, he greatly reduced the sanctions that had been imposed.

TOM DARCY
Courtesy Newsday

WHEN IT COMES TIME TO
HANG THE CAPITALISTS,
THEY WILL SELL US THE
ROPE TO DO IT. LENIN

MILT PRIGGEE
Courtesy Dayton Journal–Herald

BOB GORRELL
Courtesy Charlotte News

ROBERT SULLIVAN
Courtesy Worcester Telegram

BOB TAYLOR
Courtesy Dallas Times–Herald

EDD ULUSCHAK
Courtesy Edmonton Journal

DICK WRIGHT
*Courtesy Providence (R.I.)
Journal–Bulletin*

The E.R.A.

In 1978 a strenuous campaign by pro-Equal Rights Amendment forces had persuaded Congress to extend the deadline for ratification to June 30, 1982. The amendment needed three more states to pass the measure, but supporters failed to pick up a single one. Polls showed that a majority of the public favored ERA, but it was soundly defeated by a well-organized opposition.

ERA opponents argued that the legislation would destroy the structure of the family, end child support and alimony payments, and in general was not needed. Supporters felt that the advantages of the amendment far outweighed any disadvantages. Only two weeks after it died a natural death, the measure was introduced in Congress once again by a large bipartisan group of sponsors.

KATE SALLEY PALMER
Courtesy Greenville News

BEN SARGENT
Courtesy Austin American–Statesman

MIKE PETERS
Courtesy Dayton Daily News

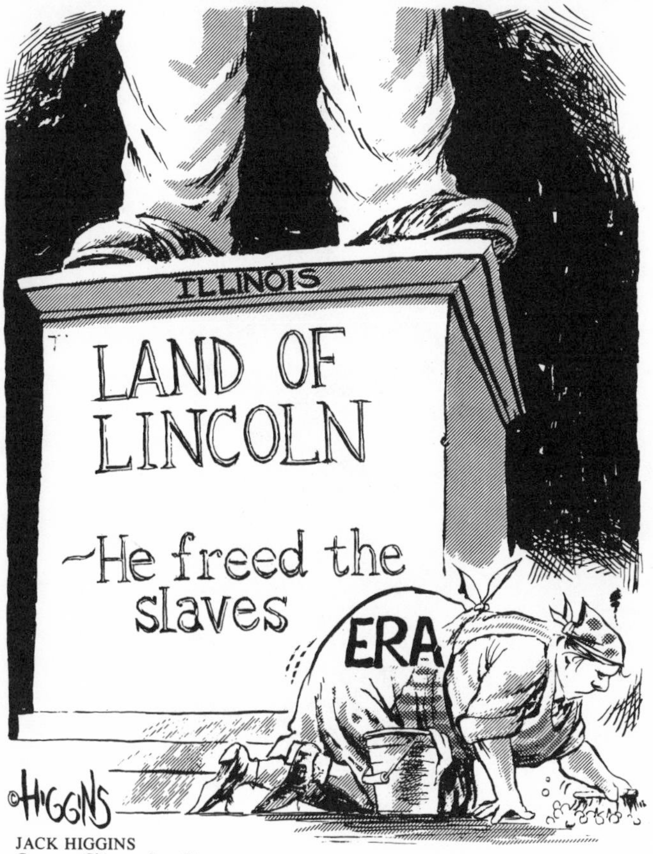
ILLINOIS
LAND OF LINCOLN
—He freed the slaves
ERA
HIGGINS

JACK HIGGINS
Courtesy Chicago Sun–Times

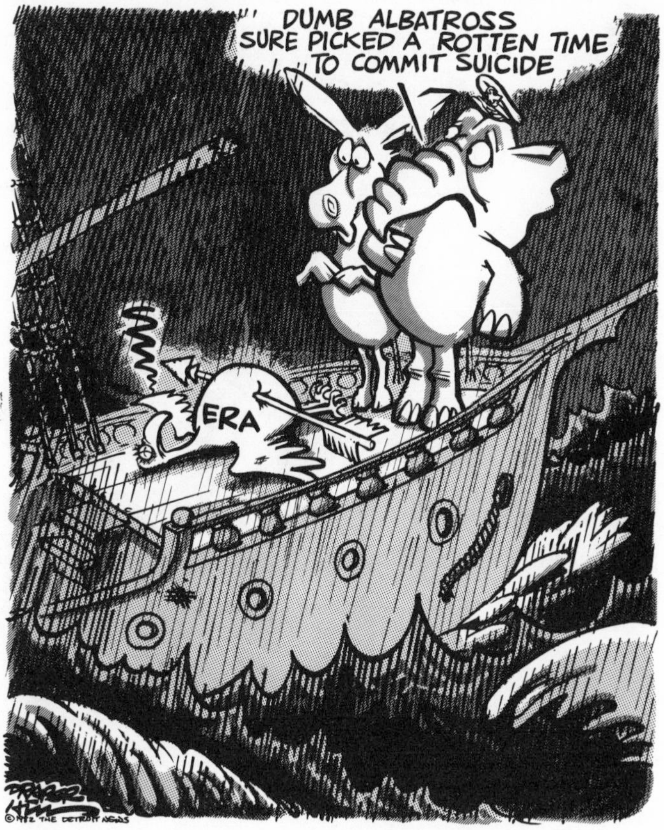
DUMB ALBATROSS SURE PICKED A ROTTEN TIME TO COMMIT SUICIDE
ERA

DRAPER HILL
Courtesy Detroit News

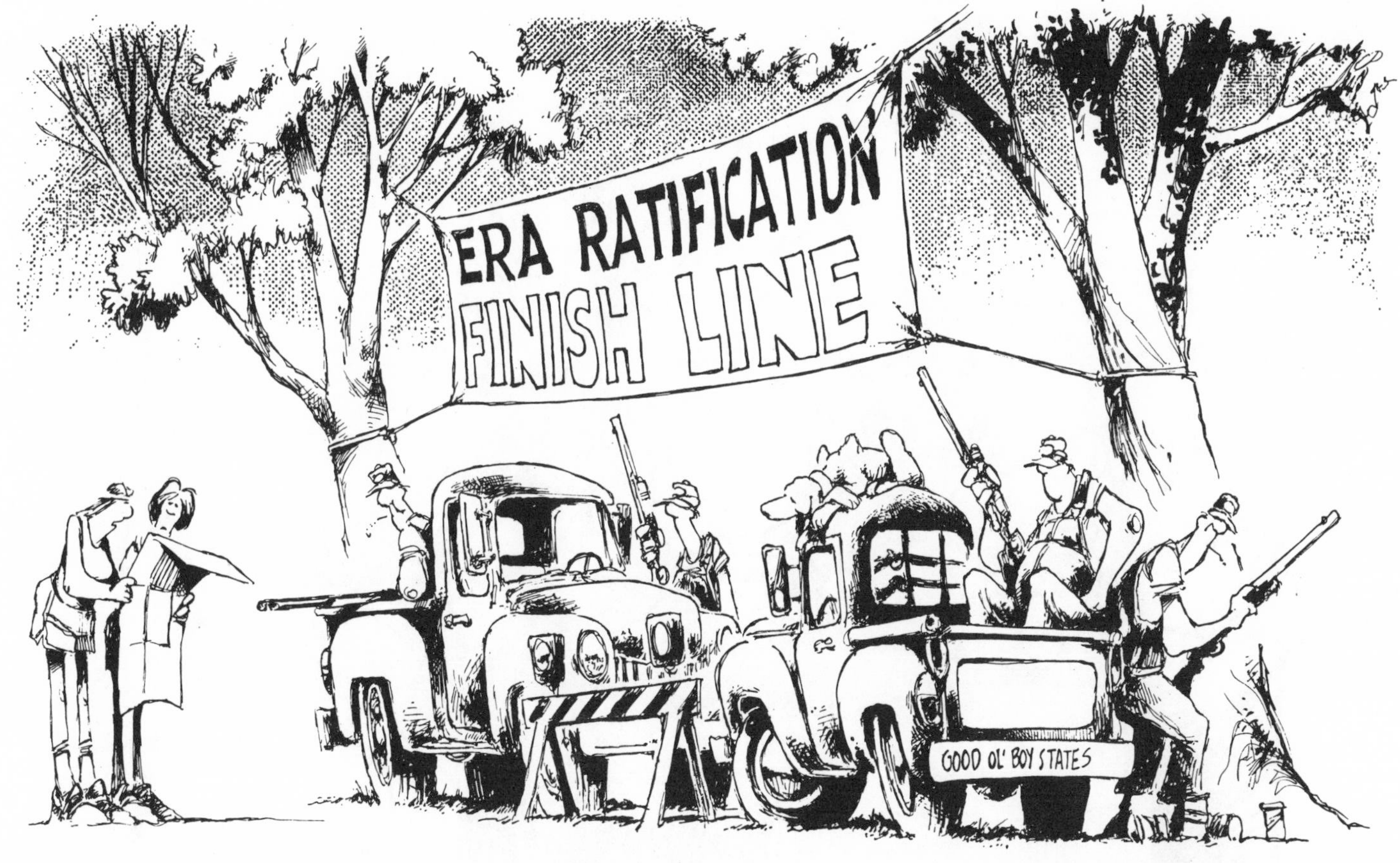
ERA RATIFICATION
FINISH LINE
GOOD OL' BOY STATES

CHAN LOWE
Courtesy Oklahoma City Times

"...there's *GOTTA* be an alternate route!"

ED GAMBLE
Courtesy Florida Times–Union

CHAN LOWE
Courtesy Oklahoma City Times

JIM BORGMAN
Courtesy Cincinnati Enquirer

JIM MAZZOTTA
Ft. Myers News–Press

JOHN BRANCH
Courtesy San Antonio Express–News

143

Pope John Paul II

Pope John Paul II continued his international travels during the year, adding five major journeys to the nine he had made previously.

He first visited West Africa; then he traveled to the well-known shrine at Fatima, Portugal, as a personal statement of gratitude for having survived the attempt on his life in 1981. As Pope John Paul walked toward the basilica in Fatima, a man lunged toward him with a bayonet, but he was seized before he could do the pontiff harm. The assailant was an archconservative Spanish priest opposed to liberal Vatican reform measures.

The Pope became the first pontiff to set foot on English soil when he traveled to Great Britain. Later in the year he paid a visit to Argentina. In a controversial move, John Paul met with Palestine Liberation Organization leader Yasir Arafat in September.

The Pope continued to express grave concern over the situation in his native Poland. He scheduled a trip to his homeland, but it was postponed without explanation. Observers believe that Pope John Paul had asked for the release of labor leader Lech Walesa and that the military government had spurned the request. The Warsaw government did agree to a visit by the Pope in 1983.

DICK WRIGHT
Courtesy Providence (R.I.)
Journal–Bulletin

CARLOS B. MALVIDO
Mexico

Excuse the yarmulka.

JOSH BEUTEL
Courtesy St. John Telegraph–Journal

ANDY DONATO
Courtesy Toronto Sun

RAY OSRIN
Courtesy Cleveland Plain Dealer

In Memoriam

A galaxy of notables passed away during 1982. Leonid Illyich Brezhnev, who had led the Soviet Union as general secretary of the Communist Party's Central Committee and as president, died on November 10 in Moscow. He had been in power since 1964.

Film star Ingrid Bergman died August 29 in London at age 67. She had achieved stardom in the 1940s for such film classics as *Casablanca*, *Gaslight*, and *For Whom the Bell Tolls*. She was a three-time Oscar winner and was posthumously awarded an Emmy for her performance as Golda Meir in a 1982 television documentary.

The Princess of Monaco, former movie star Grace Kelly, was killed in an automobile accident in France. Leroy Robert "Satchel" Paige, a legendary baseball pitcher and folk hero, died at age 75 in Kansas City, Missouri. He is credited with pitching some 2,500 games and 55 no-hitters.

Other famous personalities who died in 1982 included: Henry Fonda, 77; John Belushi, 33; Hoagy Carmichael, 82; Hans Conreid, 66; Abe Fortas, 71; Dave Garroway, 69; Archibald MacLeish, 89; Pierre Mendes-France, 75; Eleanor Powell, 69; Pete Reiser, 62; Bess Truman, 97; and King Vidor, 88.

MILT PRIGGEE
Courtesy Dayton Journal–Herald

ON GOLDEN CLOUD

DWANE POWELL
Courtesy News & Observer (N.C.)

ROGER HARVELL
Courtesy Pine Bluff Commercial

BOB ZSCHIESCHE
©Zschiesche Cartoons

147

Goodnight, Sweet Princess!

BERT WHITMAN
Courtesy Phoenix Gazette

CORKY
Courtesy Honolulu Star–Bulletin

. . . and Other Issues

A curious battle broke out among the nation's hamburger giants—McDonald's, Burger King, and Wendy's—when Burger King launched an advertising campaign intended to persuade consumers that its hamburger is bigger and better. McDonald's tried unsuccessfully to halt the campaign through legal measures, and Wendy's also got into the argument before it was over.

The price of gold fell sharply during the year. Shipments of the precious metal were off by $1.6 billion from the first six months of 1981. By late summer, however, prices had begun to climb once again as interest rates continued downward.

American farmers enjoyed record production in a number of crops, but low commodity prices, coupled with high interest rates, kept many in a real squeeze. As a result many farmers gave up agriculture for more stable livelihoods. U.S. Department of Agriculture figures showed that for the first half of 1982 prices received by farmers averaged 15 percent below costs. After adjustment for inflation, farm income for the entire year was at its lowest level since 1933.

DANA SUMMERS
Courtesy The Sentinel

MIRACLE OF LIFE

SNIVELING LITTLE
WELFARE CHEAT

TOM MEYER
Courtesy San Francisco Chronicle

JOHN CRAWFORD
Courtesy Alabama Journal

"ACTUALLY, LADY.. JUST THE RESTRAINT IS REQUIRED.... "

DOUG MACGREGOR
Courtesy Norwich Bulletin

NEWS ITEM: SCIENTISTS ARE TRYING TO DETERMINE WHAT CAUSED THE SUDDEN EXTINCTION OF DINOSAURS

BOB ENGLEHART
Courtesy Hartford Courant

KEVIN KALLAUGHER
© K.K. Syndication Service (Eng.)

How to hide from a recession

TIMOTHY ATSEFF
Courtesy Syracuse Herald-Journal

MILT PRIGGEE
Courtesy Dayton Journal–Herald

WAYNE STAYSKAL
Courtesy Chicago Tribune

"DID ANYONE GET THE NUMBER OF THAT BURGER KING DELIVERY TRUCK?"

BERT WHITMAN
Courtesy Phoenix Gazette

ART BIMROSE
Courtesy The Oregonian

CHESTER COMMODORE
Courtesy Chicago Defender

JIM ORTON
Courtesy Computerworld

153

DICK WALLMEYER
*Courtesy Independent Press–Telegram
(Calif.)*

TOMB OF THE KNOWN SOLDIER

DOUG REGALIA
Courtesy Daily Californian

ON GOLDEN POND

VERN THOMPSON
Courtesy Lawton (Okla.) Constitution

Back To The Caves

EDDIE GERMANO
Courtesy Brockton Daily Enterprise

BLAINE
Courtesy The Spectator (Ont.)

RICHARD CROWSON
Courtesy Jackson (Tenn.) Sun

ED ASHLEY
Courtesy Toledo Blade

RAY OSRIN
Courtesy Cleveland Plain Dealer

JERRY FEARING
Courtesy St. Paul Dispatch–
Pioneer Press

Past Award Winners

PULITZER PRIZE EDITORIAL CARTOON

1922—Rollin Kirby, New York World
1924—J. N. Darling, New York Herald Tribune
1925—Rollin Kirby, New York World
1926—D. R. Fitzpatrick, St. Louis Post-Dispatch
1927—Nelson Harding, Brooklyn Eagle
1928—Nelson Harding, Brooklyn Eagle
1928—Nelson Harding, Brooklyn Eagle
1929—Rollin Kirby, New York World
1930—Charles Macauley, Brooklyn Eagle
1931—Edmund Duffy, Baltimore Sun
1932—John T. McCutcheon, Chicago Tribune
1933—H. M. Talburt, Washington Daily News
1934—Edmund Duffy, Baltimore Sun
1935—Ross A. Lewis, Milwaukee Journal
1937—C. D. Batchelor, New York Daily News
1938—Vaughn Shoemaker, Chicago Daily News
1939—Charles G. Werner, Daily Oklahoman
1940—Edmund Duffy, Baltimore Sun
1941—Jacob Burck, Chicago Times
1942—Herbert L. Block, Newspaper Enterprise Association
1943—Jay N. Darling, New York Herald Tribune
1944—Clifford K. Berryman, Washington Star
1945—Bill Mauldin, United Feature Syndicate
1946—Bruce Russell, Los Angeles Times
1947—Vaughn Shoemaker, Chicago Daily News
1948—Reuben L. (Rube) Goldberg, New York Sun
1949—Lute Pease, Newark Evening News
1950—James T. Berryman, Washington Star
1951—Reginald W. Manning, Arizona Republic
1952—Fred L. Packer, New York Mirror
1953—Edward D. Kuekes, Cleveland Plain Dealer
1954—Herbert L. Block, Washington Post
1955—Daniel R. Fitzpatrick, St. Louis Post-Dispatch
1956—Robert York, Louisville Times
1957—Tom Little, Nashville Tennessean
1958—Bruce M. Shanks, Buffalo Evening News
1959—Bill Mauldin, St. Louis Post-Dispatch
1961—Carey Orr, Chicago Tribune
1962—Edmund S. Valtman, Hartford Times
1963—Frank Miller, Des Moines Register
1964—Paul Conrad, Denver Post
1966—Don Wright, Miami News
1967—Patrick B. Oliphant, Denver Post
1968—Eugene Gray Payne, Charlotte Observer
1969—John Fischetti, Chicago Daily News
1970—Thomas F. Darcy, Newsday
1971—Paul Conrad, Los Angeles Times
1972—Jeffrey K. MacNelly, Richmond News Leader
1974—Paul Szep, Boston Globe
1975—Garry Trudeau, Universal Press Syndicate
1976—Tony Auth, Philadelphia Enquirer

1977—Paul Szep, Boston Globe
1978—Jeff MacNelly, Richmond News Leader
1979—Herbert Block, Washington Post
1980—Don Wright, Miami News
1981—Herbert Block, Washington Post
1982—Ben Sargent, Austin American-Statesman

NOTE: Pulitzer Prize Award was not given 1923, 1936, 1960, 1965, and 1973.

SIGMA DELTA CHI EDITORIAL CARTOON

1942—Jacob Burck, Chicago Times
1943—Charles Werner, Chicago Sun
1944—Henry Barrow, Associated Press
1945—Reuben L. Goldberg, New York Sun
1946—Dorman H. Smith, Newspaper Enterprise Association
1947—Bruce Russell, Los Angeles Times
1948—Herbert Block, Washington Post
1949—Herbert Block, Washington Post
1950—Bruce Russell, Los Angeles Times
1951—Herbert Block, Washington Post, and
         Bruce Russell, Los Angeles Times
1952—Cecil Jensen, Chicago Daily News
1953—John Fischetti, Newspaper Enterprise Association
1954—Calvin Alley, Memphis Commercial Appeal
1955—John Fischetti, Newspaper Enterprise Association
1956—Herbert Block, Washington Post
1957—Scott Long, Minneapolis Tribune
1958—Clifford H. Baldowski, Atlanta Constitution
1959—Charles G. Brooks, Birmingham News
1960—Dan Dowling, New York Herald-Tribune
1961—Frank Interlandi, Des Moines Register
1962—Paul Conrad, Denver Post
1963—William Mauldin, Chicago Sun-Times
1964—Charles Bissell, Nashville Tennessean
1965—Roy Justus, Minneapolis Star
1966—Patrick Oliphant, Denver Post
1967—Eugene Payne, Charlotte Observer
1968—Paul Conrad, Los Angeles Times
1969—William Mauldin, Chicago Sun-Times
1970—Paul Conrad, Los Angeles Times
1971—Hugh Haynie, Louisville Courier-Journal
1972—William Mauldin, Chicago Sun-Times
1973—Paul Szep, Boston Globe
1974—Mike Peters, Dayton Daily News
1975—Tony Auth, Philadelphia Enquirer
1976—Paul Szep, Boston Globe
1977—Don Wright, Miami News
1978—Jim Borgman, Cincinnati Enquirer
1979—John P. Trever, Albuquerque Journal
1980—Paul Conrad, Los Angeles Times
1981—Paul Conrad, Los Angeles Times

NATIONAL HEADLINERS CLUB AWARD EDITORIAL CARTOON

1938—C. D. Batchelor, New York Daily News
1939—John Knott, Dallas News
1940—Herbert Block, Newspaper Enterprise Association
1941—Charles H. Sykes, Philadelphia Evening Ledger
1942—Jerry Doyle, Philadelphia Record
1943—Vaughn Shoemaker, Chicago Daily News
1944—Roy Justus, Sioux City Journal
1945—F. O. Alexander, Philadelphia Bulletin
1946—Hank Barrow, Associated Press
1947—Cy Hungerford, Pittsburgh Post-Gazette
1948—Tom Little, Nashville Tennessean
1949—Bruce Russell, Los Angeles Times
1950—Dorman Smith, Newspaper Enterprise Association
1951—C. G. Werner, Indianapolis Star
1952—John Fischetti, Newspaper Enterprise Association
1953—James T. Berryman and Gib Crockett, Washington Star
1954—Scott Long, Minneapolis Tribune
1955—Leo Thiele, Los Angeles Mirror-News
1956—John Milt Morris, Associated Press
1957—Frank Miller, Des Moines Register
1958—Burris Jenkins, Jr., New York Journal-American
1959—Karl Hubenthal, Los Angeles Examiner
1960—Don Hesse, St. Louis Globe-Democrat
1961—L. D. Warren, Cincinnati Enquirer
1962—Franklin Morse, Los Angeles Mirror
1963—Charles Bissell, Nashville Tennessean
1964—Lou Grant, Oakland Tribune
1965—Merle R. Tingley, London (Ont.) Free Press
1966—Hugh Haynie, Louisville Courier-Journal
1967—Jim Berry, Newspaper Enterprise Association
1968—Warren King, New York News
1969—Larry Barton, Toledo Blade
1970—Bill Crawford, Newspaper Enterprise Association
1971—Ray Osrin, Cleveland Plain Dealer
1972—Jacob Burck, Chicago Sun-Times
1973—Ranan Lurie, New York Times
1974—Tom Darcy, Newsday
1975—Bill Sanders, Milwaukee Journal
1976—No award given
1977—Paul Szep, Boston Globe
1978—Dwane Powell, Raleigh News and Observer
1979—Pat Oliphant, Washington Star
1980—Don Wright, Miami News
1981—Bill Garner, Memphis Commercial Appeal
1982—Mike Peters, Dayton Daily News

NATIONAL NEWSPAPER AWARD/CANADA EDITORIAL CARTOON

1949—Jack Boothe, Toronto Globe and Mail
1950—James G. Reidford, Montreal Star
1951—Len Norris, Vancouver Sun
1952—Robert La Palme, Le Devoir, Montreal
1953—Robert W. Chambers, Halifax Chronicle-Herald
1954—John Collins, Montreal Gazette
1955—Merle R. Tingley, London Free Press
1956—James G. Reidford, Toronto Globe and Mail
1957—James G. Reidford, Toronto Globe and Mail
1958—Raoul Hunter, Le Soleil, Quebec
1959—Duncan Macpherson, Toronto Star
1960—Duncan Macpherson, Toronto Star
1961—Ed McNally, Montreal Star
1962—Duncan Macpherson, Toronto Star
1963—Jan Kamienski, Winnipeg Tribune
1964—Ed McNally, Montreal Star
1965—Duncan Macpherson, Toronto Star
1966—Robert W. Chambers, Halifax Chronicle-Herald
1967—Raoul Hunter, Le Soleil, Quebec
1968—Roy Peterson, Vancouver Sun
1969—Edward Uluschak, Edmonton Journal
1970—Duncan Macpherson, Toronto Daily Star
1971—Yardley Jones, Toronto Sun
1972—Duncan Macpherson, Toronto Star
1973—John Collins, Montreal Gazette
1974—Blaine, Hamilton Spectator
1975—Roy Peterson, Vancouver Sun
1976—Andy Donato, Toronto Sun
1977—Terry Mosher, Montreal Gazette
1978—Terry Mosher, Montreal Gazette
1979—Edd Uluschak, Edmonton Journal
1980—Vic Roschkov, Toronto Star
1981—Tom Innes, Calgary Herald

JOHN FISCHETTI AWARD EDITORIAL CARTOON

1982—Lee Judge, Kansas City Times

Index

INDEX